Loving with a Vengeance

Loving with a Vengeance

MASS-PRODUCED FANTASIES
FOR WOMEN

Tania Modleski

Routledge
NEW YORK   LONDON

First published 1982 as an Archon Book,
an imprint of The Shoe String Press, Inc.,
Hamden, Connecticut 06514

First published in paperback in 1984 in the United States of America
by Methuen, Inc., 733 Third Avenue, New York, NY 10017
Published in paperback throughout the rest of world by
Methuen & Co. Ltd., 11 New Fetter Lane, London EC4P 4EE

Reprinted 1985, 1988

Reprinted in 1990 by Routledge, an imprint of Routledge, Chapman and
Hall, Inc. 39 West 35th Street, New York, NY 10001

Printed in the United States of America

Chapter II appeared in slightly altered and condensed forms in Signs:
Journal of Women in Culture and Society, Volume 5, no. 3 (Spring 1980).
Reprinted here by permission of the University of Chicago Press.
Copyright © 1980 by the University of Chicago. An abbreviated version
of Chapter IV was first published in Film Quarterly, Vol. 33, No. 1
(Fall 1979). Copyright © 1979 by the Regents of the University of
California. Reprinted by permission of The Regents.

Library of Congress Cataloging in Publication Data

Modleski, Tania, 1949–
    Loving with a vengeance.

    Bibliography: p.
    Includes index.
    1. English fiction—History and criticism. 2. Women
in literature. 3. American fiction—History and criticism.
4. Women—Books and reading. 5. Women—
Psychology. 6. Popular literature—History and criticism.
7. Soap operas—History and criticism. 8. Fantasy in
literature. I. Title.
PR830.W6M6   1984   823'.009'9287   84-14830
ISBN 0-415-90136-7 (pbk.)

British Library Cataloguing in Publication Data

Modleski, Tania
    Loving with a vengeance.

    1. English fiction—History and criticism
    2. Women—Books and reading
    I. Title
    823'.009'9287   PR830.W6

ISBN 0-415-90136-7 (pbk.)

To Nadia

Contents

Acknowledgements

I would like to thank my friends for their invaluable help on this project: Nadia Coiner, Jean Franco, Jean Friedman, Kathleen Newman, Dana Polan, and, especially, Michael Reuben whose empathy and acuteness as a reader are truly remarkable.

I

Mass-Produced Fantasies
for Women

I

Although Harlequin Romances, Gothic novels, and soap operas provide mass(ive) entertainment for countless numbers of women of varying ages, classes, and even educational backgrounds, very few critics have taken them seriously enough to study them in any detail. The double critical standard, which feminists have claimed biases literary studies, is operative in the realm of mass-culture studies as well. One cannot find any writings on popular feminine narratives to match the aggrandized titles of certain classic studies of popular male genres ("The Gangster as Tragic Hero") or the inflated claims made for, say, the detective novel which fill the pages of the *Journal of Popular Culture*. At a time when courses on popular culture have become semirespectable curricular offerings in the universities, one is often hard put to find listed on the syllabi a single novel, film, or television program which makes its appeal primarily to women. As Virginia Woolf observed some time ago, "Speaking crudely, football and sport are 'important'; the worship of fashion, the buying of clothes 'trivial.' And these values are inevitably transferred from life to fiction"—to popular fiction no less than to the fiction in the "great tradition."[1]

However, this is *not* to advocate that criticism of female popular culture should simply "plug into" categories used in studies of male popular culture, categories which are themselves often secondhand, having been borrowed from "high culture" criticism in an effort to gain respectability. Such a task would be impossible even were it desirable. As Joanna Russ has argued, the positive cultural myths are mostly male ones; role reversal (for example, "The Scheming Little Adventuress as Tragic Hero") is an impossibility, involving a contradiction in terms.[2]

There are no doubt a number of reasons why female protagonists and female popular fiction cannot claim for themselves the kind of status male heroes and male texts so often claim. This kind of aggrandizement, occurring both in fiction and in criticism, would appear to be a masculine mode, traceable, at least in part, to the male oedipal conflict. This conflict, it is important to note, is resolved at the expense of woman and necessitates her devaluation. For the male gains access to culture and the symbolic first by perceiving the "lack" of the once all-powerful mother and then by identifying with the "superior" male, the father. Recently, critics, following Roland Barthes, have plausibly argued that most popular or "classic" narratives reenact the male oedipal crisis.[3] We need not list here the dreary catalogue of devices used in the male text to disable the female and thus assert masculine superiority (the grapefruit mashed in the woman's face by one "tragic hero"). At the end of a majority of popular narratives the woman is disfigured, dead, or at the very least, domesticated. And *her* downfall is seen as anything *but* tragic. There are other ways in which male texts work to insist implicitly on their difference from the feminine. Sometimes this is done through language: for instance, through rigorous suppression of "flowery" descriptions or the tight-lipped refusal to employ any expression of emotion other than anger.

Criticism, too, finds it necessary to enhance the superiority of its objects: the male hero and the male text. The temptation to elevate what men do simply because men do it is, it would seem, practically irresistible. (Freud himself succumbed to it. As Kenneth Burke points out, Freud, in his efforts to deflate the ego's pretensions, to show what ignoble fears and shameful desires lurk beneath the beauties of civilization, wound up glorifying these fears and desires by invoking Oedipus, one of the most grandiose figures of Western myth: The-Little-Man-Fearing-For-His-"Widdler" as Tragic Hero.)[4] Further, criticism, like the text itself, often raises its object at the expense of the feminine. Not only does the critical equation of pen and penis, discussed by Sandra Gilbert and Susan Gubar in *The Madwoman in the Attic*, suggest that women lack the necessary equipment to write, or at least to write well, but the feminine text itself is often used as a standard by which other products are measured and found to be not wanting. How often have we seen soap operas used in this way? Even as serious and sensitive a critic of mass culture as Raymond Williams can write, "Since their origins in commercial radio in the thirties, many serials have been dismissed as 'soap opera'. Yet . . ." And the implication, borne out in the rest of the paragraph, is that a necessary if not a sufficient criterion for the worth of serials is their difference from the (utterly dismissable) soap operas.[5]

Given this pervasive scorn for all things feminine, it is hardly surprising that since the beginnings of the novel the heroine and the writer of feminine texts have been on the defensive, operating on the constant assumption that men are out to destroy them. In the earliest plots the heroine was forced to protect her social reputation against the seducer who would rob her of this most prized possession. Similarly, the woman writer worked to protect her literary reputation against the dastardly critics. To aid her heroine in the protection of her virtue the writer, like male authors but for different reasons, had to disable her: e.g. to render her entirely ignorant of the most basic facts of life so that the man, finally impressed by her purity, would quit trying to destroy her and would, instead, reward and elevate her—i.e. marry her. What is worse, in her anxiety to ward off critical scorn, the woman writer had to disable *herself*, to proclaim her weakness and ignorance loudly and clearly, hoping to be "mercifully spared." One fairly typical preface reads:

> When I attempt to interest an impartial Public in favour
> of the following Work, it is not from a vain hope, that it
> is deserving of the *approbation* of the *judicious*. —No,
> my hopes are better founded; a candid, a liberal, a gen-
> erous Public will make the necessary allowances for the
> *first* attempt of a young female Adventurer in Letters.[6]

Thus, if self-aggrandizement has been the male mode, self-abasement has too frequently been the female mode.

As if this were not enough, the criticism written by women has long been in the habit of denigrating what George Eliot called "Silly Novels by Lady Novelists."[7] Of course, plenty of male critics spurn silly novels written by either sex, but their criticism never seems to be so personally motivated. Eliot, for example, wrote her essay out of concern that men would find in these novels proof of the universal inability of women to write anything *but* silly works. Thus women's criticism was also often written out of self-defensiveness and the fear of men's power to destroy.

Heroines of contemporary popular narratives for women continue to act defensively, and if their writers are no longer apol-

13

ogizing for their activity, women critics are more than ever uncomfortable with these narratives. Such discomfort is, to a certain extent, justified, but what is most striking is that it too seems to manifest a defensiveness which has not been felt through. Whereas the old (and some of the new) heroines have to protect themselves against the seductions of the hero, feminist critics seem to be strenuously disassociating themselves from the seductiveness of the feminine texts. And whereas the heroine of romance, as we shall see, turns against her own better self, the part of her which feels anger at men, the critic turns against her own "worse" self, the part of her which has not yet been "liberated" from shameful fantasies.

Thus women's criticism of popular feminine narratives has generally adopted one of three attitudes: dismissiveness; hostility —tending unfortunately to be aimed at the consumers of the narratives; or, most frequently, a flippant kind of mockery.[8] This is the tone used by Eliot, with whom one does not usually associate it. It is, significantly, indistinguishable from the tone men often use when they mention feminine popular art. Again, the ridicule is certainly to some extent justified (though no more justified than it would be if aimed at much male popular art), but it often seems to betray a kind of *self*-mockery, a fear that someone will think badly of the writer for even touching on the subject, however gingerly. In assuming this attitude, we demonstrate not so much our freedom from romantic fantasy as our acceptance of the critical double standard and of the masculine contempt for sentimental (feminine) "drivel." Perhaps we have internalized the ubiquitous male spy, who watches as we read romances or view soap operas, as he watched Virginia Woolf from behind the curtain (or so she suspected) when she delivered her subversive lectures at "Oxbridge," or as he intently observes the romantic heroine just when she thinks she is alone and free at last to be herself.

The present work was conceived and undertaken out of concern that these narratives were not receiving the right kind of attention. I try to avoid expressing either hostility or ridicule, to get beneath the embarrassment, which I am convinced provokes both the anger and the mockery, and to explore the reasons for the deep-rooted and centuries-old appeal of the narratives. Their enormous and continuing popularity, I assume, suggests that they speak to very real problems and tensions in women's lives. The narrative strategies which have evolved for smoothing over these tensions can tell us much about how women have managed not only to live in oppressive circumstances but to invest their situations with some degree of dignity.

Although there have been few serious or detailed studies of contemporary mass art for women, popular feminine narratives of the eighteenth and nineteenth centuries have received much more attention. Some scholars have pointed to the enormous influence of these older narratives on contemporary life and letters. Ann Douglas, for example, holds the nineteenth-century novels by and for women responsible for many of the evils of mass culture. Discussing Little Eva of *Uncle Tom's Cabin* as a typical "narcissistic" heroine, Douglas says, "Stowe's infantile heroine anticipates that exaltation of the average which is the trademark of mass culture." And further, "The pleasure Little Eva gave me provided historical and practical preparation for the equally indispensable and disquieting comforts of mass culture."[9] Although I think this is going a bit far, the more modest claim that early popular novels for women anticipate the narratives which women find compelling in the twentieth century is certainly demonstrable. Therefore, the debates which even now surround the early narratives (what was their worth? what function did they serve?) are of relevance to any consideration of the later ones.

II

To introduce an admittedly overschematized lineage for the three forms under consideration, Harlequins can be traced back through the work of Charlotte Brontë and Jane Austen to the sentimental novel and ultimately, as I shall have more than one occasion to note, to the novels of Samuel Richardson, whose *Pamela* is considered by many scholars to be the first British novel (it was also the first English novel printed in America); Gothic romances for women, also traceable through Charlotte Brontë, date back to the eighteenth century and the work of Ann Radcliffe; and soap operas are descendants of the domestic novels and the sensation novels of the nineteenth century. In turn, the "antecedants" of the domestic novels, according to Nina Baym, "lay . . . in the novel of manners, with its 'mixed' heroine as developed by Fanny Burney, and even more in the fiction of the English women moralists—Mrs. Opie, Mrs. Barbauld, and especially Maria Edgeworth, with her combination of educational intention, moral fabulating, and description of manners and customs."[10]

My classification is, as I say, overschematized, for the genres do overlap. Thus the plot of the sentimental novel, which often depicts a young, innocent woman defending her virginity against the attacks of a rake, who might or might not reform, would frequently find its way into the domestic novel, which tended to center around women's activities in the home. The following is a description of the routine of the heroine of Susan Warner's enormously popular *Queechy*:

> By the most conservative estimate, Fleda performed the parts of three hired men, cook, dairy manager, nurse, and teacher. Up before dawn to do the chores and to care for the livestock, she found time before breakfast to study the latest agricultural methods by which she turned a run-down farm into the show place of the county. The produce from her truck garden commanded the highest prices at market and her new method of haying resulted in the banner crop of the year. In addition to the cares involved in these enterprises, she blacked the boots of her numerous guests, revived the drooping health of an ailing family, and improved her mind by reading and study. Her leisure moments, which were necessarily limited, were spent in dodging the persistent efforts of the villainous Thorn, who devoted his full time to plotting her seduction![11]

Here is a very potent feminine fantasy, common to most nineteenth-century novels and to their twentieth-century counterparts. The man, whether he is plotting the woman's seduction or, as in soap operas, endlessly discussing his marital woes with his coworkers at the hospital, spends all his time thinking about the woman. Even when he appears most indifferent to her, as he frequently does in Harlequin Romances, we can be sure he will eventually tell her how much the thought of her has obsessed him. Thus, women writers have always had their own way of "evening things up" between men and women, even when they seemed most fervently to embrace their subordinate status.

The sentimental novel flourished in America at the end of the eighteenth and in the early nineteenth century. It was, however, an

English import rather than an indigenous American product. Like the Harlequins of the present day, the novels repeatedly insisted on the importance of the heroine's virginity. In the classic formula, the heroine, who is often of lower social status than the hero, holds out against his attacks on her "virtue" until he sees no other recourse than to marry her. Of course, by this time he wants to marry her, having become smitten with her sheer "goodness." The early women novelists became preoccupied, not to say obsessed, with the morality of this plot. Whether or not a rake would really reform was a burning question: some novelists said no, some said yes, and many said no and yes—i.e. put themselves on record as being opposed to the idea that a rake would ever improve his morals and then proceeded to make an exception of their hero.

In these debates, however, the sexual double standard was seldom seriously challenged; very few women went so far as one female character, who, in any case, is not the heroine of the novel: "I could never see the propriety of the assertion [that reformed rakes make the best husbands]. Might it not be said with equal justice, that if a certain description of females were reformed, they would make the best wives?"[12] Rather, the inequality between the sexes was dealt with in other ways. According to J.M.S. Tompkins, for instance, the effect of the "cult of sensibility," the belief that people are innately good and that this goodness is demonstrated in elaborate displays of feeling, "was to induce some measure of approximation in the ethical ideals and emotional sensitiveness of the two sexes." Approval was therefore given to the hero who exhibited an "almost feminine sensibility."[13] In Harlequins, the battle continues to be fought out not in the sexual arena, but in the emotional and—stretching the term—the ethical one. If the Harlequin heroine never questions the necessity of remaining a virgin while the man is allowed to have had a variety of sexual experiences, there is a tacit insistence that the man share her "values." In other words, "speaking crudely," the novels literally reverse the hierarchy pointed out by Virginia Woolf, for "the worship of fashion, the buying of clothes" are important—to both the woman and the man, who is usually even capable of identifying a material as "tulle." More, in novel after novel, the man is brought to acknowledge the preeminence of love and the attractions of domesticity at which he has, as a rule, previously scoffed.

Another typical, but far more somber plot, dealt with the woman who gave in to the libertine, and at the end of the novel died a penitent and often excruciating death. This is essentially the story of the two most popular women's novels of the period, Susanna Rowson's *Charlotte: A Tale of Truth* and Hannah Webster Foster's *The Coquette*. If the reformed-rake plot is borrowed from *Pamela*, the novel of seduction is indebted to *Clarissa*, though, significantly, the women novelists allowed their heroines some measure of conscious choice in their "fall," whereas Clarissa, after her initial error of leaving the family, remained pure and had to be drugged to be deprived of her "virtue." The emotional force of these novels seems often to lie less in the act of sin, the "elopement," than in the death scenes themselves, a fact which has disturbed and puzzled many critics. But death is too convenient to women fantasists to be easily relinquished, for it can serve a variety of functions. On the one hand, it endows the woman with something like "tragic hero" status: "What can a heroine do?" asks Joanna Russ in pointing out that men have taken all the active plots.[14] She can die. And in dying, she does not have to depart from the passive feminine role, but only logically extend it. On the other hand, death can be a very powerful means of wreaking vengeance on others who do not properly "appreciate" us, and it is in this form that the fantasy of death can be found in Harlequin Romances, which, with their happy endings, seem on the surface to have nothing in common with the tragic *Clarissa* plot.

From one point of view nothing could be easier than to ridicule the prevalence of the seducer in these early novels, and scholars, especially male scholars, have not been behindhand in doing so. Carl Van Doren writes, "Modern readers might think that age one of the most illicit on record if they did not understand that Richardson's Lovelace is merely being repeated in different colors and proportions."[15] But even in popular literature, it is never a question of "mere" repetition; why, for example, did women writers not choose to "repeat" Tom Jones or Humphrey Clinker? The figures of Mr. B. in *Pamela*, Lovelace in *Clarissa*, together with their numerous successors, enhanced the importance of women (for the men spend their full time "plotting the seductions" of the heroines) and at the same time provide the means by which women can localize their diffuse and general sense of powerlessness.

In giving vent to this sense of powerlessness, the sentimental novels look forward to the themes, fantasies, and preoccupations of both the domestic novels and the Gothic novels. The "reformed-rake" plot and the debate which raged around it pointed to women's sense of vulnerability in regard to marriage and hence foreshadowed the critique of the family which would be the covert project of the so-called "domestic" novelists. As Foster's *The Coquette* makes clear, one of the great attractions of the rake was that he seemed to provide an exciting alternative to the staid domestic "pleasures" which were all good women were supposed to want. Eliza Warton, the ultimately ruined heroine, continually puts off her rather dull clerical suitor in the hopes of receiving a more interesting offer from the lively and witty libertine, Peter Sanford. She complains:

> I recoil at the thought of immediately forming a connec-
> tion, which must confine me to the duties of domestic
> life, and make me dependent for happiness, perhaps
> too, for subsistence, upon a class of people, who will
> claim the right of scrutinizing every part of my conduct;
> and by censuring those foibles, which I am conscious of
> not having prudence to avoid, may render me complete-
> ly miserable.[16]

But, of course, marrying a rake could lead to even more serious domestic disasters; thus, a number of novels showed women marrying men of less than "sound moral principle" and subsequently portrayed the husbands "dragging their families into debt and disgrace and violently closing the scene with suicide."[17] At their extreme, such fears inevitably lead to paranoia: "God bless you, my child," exclaims the mother of one "sentimental" heroine, "be careful, circumspect, and wary; suspect every one of a design on you till you are convinced of the contrary. You must think all men knaves and all women treacherous, and then you will avoid many troubles. Trust no one. . . ."[18] As we shall see, Gothic novels most fully express this paranoid sense of the world and, furthermore, help women to come to terms with the mothers who (as in the above quotation) seem to be responsible for passing on this paranoia to their daughters in a world ruled by men.

The Gothic novels of Horace Walpole, Ann Radcliffe, and Matthew Lewis achieved their peak of popularity in America at about the same time as the sentimental novel. Critics often attribute their immense popularity to the public's desire for "mere" entertainment. James Hart's *The Popular Book: A History of America's Literary Taste* succinctly concludes that many people found in these novels "a new form of escape from their own humdrum lives, allowing them vicariously to experience thrilling adventures. From the middle class of America to the Middle Ages of Europe was a wonderfully exciting journey, when made through the medium of a Gothic novel."[19] However, it is possible to see the exotic settings of Gothics as possessing a much more important function: because the novels so radically displace reality by putting the action in distant times and strange and ghostly lands, they are uniquely equipped to become a site for the displacement of repressed wishes and fears. In other words, Gothics can present us with the frighteningly familiar precisely because they make the familiar strange—which is, it will be recalled, the way Freud said the uncanny sensation in literature is produced. Thus, set in a remote place, in a faraway time, the female Gothic as created by Ann Radcliffe in *The Mysteries of Udolpho* expresses women's most intimate fears, or, more precisely, their fears about intimacy—about the exceedingly private, even claustrophobic nature of their existence. So it is that the house, the building itself, to which women are generally confined in real life, becomes the locus of evil in an entirely make-believe sixteenth-century Italian mountain setting.

Furthermore, female Gothics provide an outlet for women's fears about fathers and husbands, fears which are much more pronounced than the sentimental heroine's. The plot of Radcliffe's *The Mysteries of Udolpho*, on which the later Gothic novels are based, has a villainous Montoni carrying off the heroine Emily and her aunt, whom Montoni marries for her fortune, to a castle in the mountains where he imprisons the aunt and persecutes the niece in order to gain control of her fortune. I will argue that this plot became popular at a time when the nuclear family was being consolidated in part because it portrayed in an extremely exaggerated form a family dynamic which would increasingly become the norm. It spoke powerfully to the young girl struggling to achieve psychological autonomy in a home where the remote, but all-powerful father ruled over an utterly dependent wife.

In a sense, then, Gothics are "domestic" novels too, concerned with the (often displaced) relationships among family members and with driving home to women the importance of coping with enforced confinement and the paranoid fears it generates. Thus, although nineteenth-century readers soon dropped Gothic novels in favor of the "domestic novels," it could be argued that the later novels are somewhat continuous with the earlier ones. Indeed, Jane

Austen, preeminent among novelists of manners, who antedated the domestic novelists, began her career not simply burlesquing the Gothic tradition, but extracting its core of truth: her mercenary and domineering General Tilney of *Northanger Abbey* may not be capable of imprisoning his wife in a turret, but, like the Gothic villain, he *is* capable of rendering her existence entirely miserable, and of coldly ruining the heroine's hopes for happiness.

After dying out for over a century, Gothic novels again became popular upon publication in 1938 of Daphne Du Maurier's *Rebecca*, a novel about a woman marrying a man whom she subsequently suspects of still being in love with his (dead) first wife, but who, it turns out, has actually murdered the wife out of anger at her promiscuity. Significantly, this second "Gothic revival" took place at the same time that "hard-boiled" detective novels were attracting an unprecedented number of male readers. While Dashiell Hammett and Raymond Chandler were persistently scapegoating women (in Chandler's *Farewell, My Lovely*, a woman named Helen Grayle is at the bottom of the whole sordid affair!), the paranoid fears of women were receiving new life. In the forties, a new movie genre derived from Gothic novels appeared around the time that hard-boiled detective fiction was being transformed by the medium into what movie critics currently call "film noir." Not surprisingly, film noir has received much critical scrutiny both here and abroad, while the so-called "gaslight" genre has been virtually ignored. According to many critics, film noir possesses the greatest sociological importance (in addition to its aesthetic importance) because it reveals male paranoid fears, developed during the war years, about the independence of women on the homefront. Hence the necessity in these movies of destroying or taming the aggressive, mercenary, sexually dynamic "femme fatale" whose presence is indispensable to the genre. Beginning with Alfred Hitchcock's 1940 movie version of *Rebecca* and continuing through and beyond George Cukor's *Gaslight* in 1944, the gaslight films may be seen to reflect *women's* fears about losing their unprecedented freedoms and being forced back into the homes after the men returned from fighting to take over the jobs and assume control of their families. In many of these films, the house seems to be alive with menace, and the greedy, sadistic men who rule them are often suspected of trying to drive their wives insane, or to murder them as they have murdered other women in the past. The fact that after the war years these films gradually faded from the screen probably reveals more about the changing composition of movie audiences than about the waning of women's anxieties concerning domesticity. For Gothic novels have continued to this day to enjoy a steady popularity, and a few of their authors, like Victoria Holt and Mary Stewart, reliably appear on the best-seller list.

By far, the most popular form of literature for women throughout most of the nineteenth century were the "domestic novels." These novels and the sensation fiction of the 1860s, mostly from England, come together to form the prototypes of the modern soap opera. Elaine Showalter credits sensation writers with a subversive appeal, claiming that they inverted "the stereotypes of the domestic novel." Certainly the sensationalists "expressed female anger, frustration, and sexual energy more directly than had been done previously."[20] Nevertheless, several important studies by women scholars have shown that the domestic novel itself was subversive, thus challenging the orthodox view of the genre, advanced by Herbert Brown: "The domestic novels in which these writers sought to glorify the American home were as limited in scope as the narrow sphere of interests of the women readers for whom they were designed. . . . Domestic fiction records few instances of discontent with this circumscribed life."[21] James Hart corroborates Brown's assessment when he speaks of the women novelists as "middle-class ladies . . . busy fashioning their homes into the land of the heart's content."[22] In sharp contrast, Helen Waite Papashvily characterizes the novels as "handbooks . . . of feminine revolt," encouraging "a pattern of feminine behavior so quietly ruthless, so subtly vicious that by comparison the ladies at Seneca appear angels of innocence."[23] How is it possible for people to read the same group of books and come up with such wildly divergent ideas about them? The answer, I believe, is that many critics tend to take at face value the novelists' endorsement of the domestic ideal and ignore the actual, not very flattering portraits of domesticity which emerge from their works. To be sure, as Brown notes, the novelists tended strenuously to affirm the sacredness of the marriage tie, but they were concerned primarily to show how far short of the ideal many marriages in real life tended to fall. Some of the very titles of the fiction of Mrs. E.D.E.N. Southworth, one of the most prolific and popular writers of the age, suggest the grievances against marriage, fathers, and husbands Brown says are nowhere to be found: *The Fatal Vow, The Discarded Daughter, The Deserted Wife.* Nina Baym, who is more moderate than Papashvily in her account of the novels, even takes issue with the term "domestic," which she says reinforces the stereotyped idea that the novelists wallowed in domestic bliss. On the contrary, in this fiction

> home life is presented, overwhelmingly, as unhappy. There are very few intact families in this literature, and those that are intact are unstable or locked into routines of misery. Domestic tasks are arduous and monotonous; family members oppress and abuse each other; social interchanges are alternately insipid or malicious.[24]

In much "domestic" fiction men are the culprits responsible for the intense suffering of wives and daughters. Mrs. Southworth, in particular, delighted in portraying men as tyrannical, foolish, untrusting and untrustworthy. In a typical Southworth plot, the heroine is forced to fend for herself because a guardian, father, or husband persecutes or neglects her, and she manages splendidly until at the end she gets a mate worthy of her, or, alternatively, the mate she has finally comes to appreciate her virtues and abilities, and is transformed into a model husband. Similarly, Fleda's astonishing activities in *Queechy* are necessitated by her guardian's abdication of responsibility; failing in business he becomes increasingly morose, helpless, and tyrannical and ultimately abandons his family and lands them in debt.

Soap operas continue the tradition of portraying strong women who, if they no longer single-handedly run large farms, nevertheless must struggle to keep intact the worlds which the weakness and unreliability of men threaten to undermine. However, men in soap operas tend not to be the bullying tyrants frequently found in domestic fiction. The evil "villain" in soap opera is generally female, and in this respect soap opera closely resembles the nineteenth-century sensation novels written by and for women. In the fiction of Mary Louise Braddon and the recently discovered "thrillers" of Louisa May Alcott, the happiness of the "good" woman is jeopardized by the infernal machinations of a clever and beautiful temptress who gains control over the hapless man with ridiculous ease. In the chapter on soap operas I will explore the appeal of such a character and show that this plot is not really the "inversion" of the "domestic" plot but its complement. Soap operas may also be indebted to the sensation novels for the emphasis on violence, crime, and sexual scandal.

The so-called woman's film of the 1930s and 40s clearly derived from domestic fiction while it added some new themes. The stock figures of domestic fiction—the strong and brave heroines, the weak, often dissolute men—abound in the woman's film. In *Letter from an Unknown Woman,* to cite a famous example of the genre, Joan Fontaine has a brief affair with Louis Jordan, conceives a child by him, and continues to love him over the years though she marries someone else. When the two come together after a long time, he has forgotten her completely, having meanwhile been casually involved with many women. Only when she dies does he become aware of the magnificence of her nature. In *Now, Voyager* Bette Davis falls in love with Paul Henreid, who is trapped in a marriage with a selfish, hypochondriacal woman. Davis rejects a suitor and, relinquishing any hope for "a home of her own, a man of her own, a child of her own," devotes herself entirely to bringing up Henreid's child. A new twist has been given to a typical theme of domestic fiction: in the nineteenth-century novels, women had been preoccupied with children, especially children who died young. This preoccupation has been attributed to the relatively high infant mortality rate and the need of writers like Stowe, the creator of Little Eva, to make perfect martyrs out of the doomed infants. In the woman's film, on the other hand, it is the mothers or the mother-surrogates who are the martyrs, sacrificing everything for their (often ungrateful) children. This shift in attitude may be explained by the fact that women in the twentieth century, much more than their nineteenth-century counterparts, have had to depend on their children for fulfillment, since the "support networks" of women have virtually disappeared. This increased dependency generates increased resentment, a dilemma reflected in the child obsession of the woman's film as well as in soap operas.

Not only did the domestic novels call into question the felicity women were supposed to experience in making home-life the center of their existence, but they also revealed, as Papashvily shows, covert longings for power and revenge. Papashvily devotes a whole chapter of her book to "The Mutilation of the Male," a device which allows the heroine to lead a more active life than would be possible if she had a whole and healthy male to protect her, and which moreover, one suspects, served as a covert expression of feminine anger at male power. Another common device was to have the heroine married off to a man towards whom she felt nothing, but who loved her ardently, passionately, constantly.

Sometimes, self-mutilation brought about the desired masculine punishment: in the Elsie Dinsmore books, Elsie, commanded by her father to play the piano on the Sabbath, "sat at the piano until she fainted, striking her head as she fell. Her father's repentence and grief was abject enough to please the most demanding."[25]

Clearly these methods are not, as we say today, the "healthiest" means of venting anger. On the other hand, it should be heartening to feminists to know that, contrary to many male critics, women writers of popular fiction have indeed registered protest against the authority of fathers and husbands even while they appeared to give their wholehearted consent to it. Critics like Papashvily have thus performed in the realm of popular art a liberating task akin to the one engaged in by feminist critics of "high" art. Elaine Showalter beautifully describes this critical activity:

> There is an optical illusion which can be seen as either a goblet or two profiles. The images oscillate in their tension before us, one alternately superseding the other and reducing it to meaningless background. In the purest feminist literary criticism we are similarly presented with a radical alteration of our vision, a demand that we see meaning in what has previously been empty space. The orthodox plot recedes, and another plot, hitherto submerged in the anonymity of the background, stands out in bold relief like a thumbprint.[26]

Not surprisingly this hidden plot often reveals buried anger or hostility (for example, Jane Eyre's fury at Rochester's highhandedness), but it is not simply the obtuseness of male critics which has prevented the discernment of the alternate plots; these plots have had to be "submerged" into more orthodox ones just as feminine rage itself, blocked in direct expression, has had to be submerged, subterranean, devious.

In the following chapters, I will show that even the contemporary mass-produced narratives for women contain elements of protest and resistance underneath highly "orthodox" plots. This is *not* to say that the tensions, anxieties, and anger which pervade these works are solved in ways which would please modern feminists: far from it. Indeed, just as the eighteenth- and nineteenth-century popular novels for women despised and caricatured the "new woman," so too do the contemporary narratives tend to ridicule the "woman's libber" who rejects the adequacy of Bette Davis's "home of her own, man of her own, child of her own" (demanding first and foremost a "room of her own" apart from the man and the child). But, significantly, Bette Davis ultimately rejected them too, if not in favor of a career, then at least for the sake of an emotion and an ideal that transcended the alleged desires of the majority of women. If the popular-culture heroine and the feminist choose utterly different ways of overcoming their dissatisfaction, they at least have in common the dissatisfaction.

III

Objections will arise. Many critics will argue that there are crucial differences between the popular art of the nineteenth century and the mass-produced art consumed by millions today. The division between popular art and great art was not absolute then, as it is now, and popular writers not as severely controlled; hence a writer like Harriet Beecher Stowe could protest the conditions of her age in a way no longer imaginable. Today, the argument runs, only two types of art exist: mass art, which is used by its producers to manipulate the people and to "colonize" their leisure time [27]—in short, to keep them contented with the "status quo"—and high art, which is the last preserve of an autonomous, critical spirit. Since mass art is completely dominated by the "consciousness industry"[28] and since high art alone resists such domination, it follows that the responsible, socially concerned critic must continually focus his or her attention upon the differences between the two types of art. "The division itself is the truth," Max Horkheimer and T.W. Adorno asserted.[29]

This argument, first advanced by the Marxist-oriented members of the Frankfurt School (notably, Horkheimer, Adorno, and Herbert Marcuse) is especially pernicious because it makes contempt for mass art a politically progressive attitude. It is one of the great ironies in the development of mass-culture theory that the people who were first responsible for pointing out the political importance of mass art simultaneously provided the justification for slighting it. Fortunately, some recent Marxist critics have begun to challenge the assumptions of the Frankfurt School; and many of their theoretical insights inform the pages of this book.[30] Fredric

Jameson's important essay, "Reification and Utopia in Mass Culture," makes a two-pronged attack on some of the main ideas of the Frankfurt School. In the first place, he shows that high art—the "modernism" valorized by the Frankfurt School and, more recently, by the *Tel Quel* group in France—has not remained apart from the processes of the "commodification of art." For instance, although modernism may have arisen out of a desire "not to be a commodity," the very effort of avoiding the repetition and "standardization"[31] characteristic of mass art means that modernism must stress "innovation and novelty," must, therefore, capitulate to the "pressure . . . to 'make it new'" and thus act in accordance "with the ever swifter historicity of consumer society, with its yearly or quarterly style and fashion changes."[32]

More important for our purposes is the other half of Jameson's argument, which is the one he most fully develops. If, on the one hand, high art does not represent an absolute, uncompromised alternative to mass art, on the other hand, mass art may be said to possess some of the negative, critical functions the Frankfurt School and its numerous followers have attributed to high art alone. This is true on the most general level. As Hans Robert Jauss points out in a critique of Adorno's theories, every work of art presupposes "an aesthetic distance on the part of the spectator; that is, it presupposes a negation of the immediate interests of his everyday life."[33] But as Jameson shows, mass art often contains many specific criticisms of everyday life, in addition to this rather global "negation" (which, however, was of the utmost importance in the Frankfurt School's philosophy of art). As opposed to those critics who claim that mass art is designed to create "false anxieties," manipulate "false needs," and impose "false consciousness," Jameson argues that mass culture performs "a transformational work on [real] social and political anxieties and fantasies which must then have some effective presence in the mass cultural text in order subsequently to be 'managed' or repressed." He invokes the theories of Norman Holland, who in *The Dynamics of Literary Response* describes the operations of the text in producing aesthetic gratification: at the same time that the text symbolically fulfills our wishes, it must protect against the fears which "powerful archaic desires" always threaten to call forth from the unconscious. Jameson concludes:

Hence Holland's suggestive conception of the vocation

of art to *manage* this raw material of the drives and the archaic wish or fantasy material. To rewrite the concept of a management of desire in social terms now allows us to think repression and wish-fulfillment together within the unity of a single mechanism which gives and takes alike in a kind of psychic compromise or horse-trading, which strategically arouses fantasy content within careful symbolic containment structures which defuse it, gratifying intolerable, unrealizable, properly imperishable desires only to the degree to which they can be laid to rest.[34]

Jameson is right to claim that his discussion leads us some distance away from the concept of mass art as "manipulation," as "sheer brainwashing." Nevertheless, there are problems with this part of his essay, specifically with his notion of the social "management of desire," which suggests that there is someone doing the managing. Indeed, in his remarks on *The Godfather*, which Jameson uses as a test case for his theory, he speaks of the "intent to mystify," thus conjuring up, like the text itself, a sort of "Godfather" on whom to project blame.[35] Jameson and other left-wing critics of mass culture are the latest heirs to the old reformist/ Populist belief in a group of conspirators ruthlessly holding us back from the attainment of a golden age. Ironically, it is the politically conservative mass-culture critic who has on occasion warned against the tendency, as Leo Spitzer puts it, to "oversimplify the psychology of the advertiser [and, by extension, of any other so-called captain of consciousness[36]]—who is not only a businessman but a human being: one who is endowed with all the normal potentialities of emotion and who finds expression of these in the exercise of his profession."[37] More recently, European Marxists like Louis Althusser have opposed the facile assumption that there are two groups of people—those within ideology (the masses of people) and those on the outside who, without illusions themselves, manage to control the others by feeding them illusions. We are all "inside" ideology, Althusser has persuasively argued.[38]

Therefore, while my analyses support Jameson's theory that mass-cultural texts both stimulate and allay social anxieties, both arouse and symbolically satisfy the "properly imperishable" desires and fantasies of women, I avoid imputing to, for example, the board of directors of the Harlequin Company, an omniscience about the nature and effects of their product. I sincerely doubt that the men on the board, cynical as they may be about feminine romance, actually possess a total awareness of where "mystification" leaves off and "truth" begins. Indeed, I am quite sure that any cynicism they feel is derived from a mystification of what it means to be a male: *viz.* a "superior" being with "higher" interests and values. This masculine attitude may in fact drive women to Harlequins for a "false" solution to the anxieties it creates, but that is because it is an attitude shared by most men.

The work of Althusser, itself influenced by the psychoanalytic thought of Jacques Lacan, has spurred renewed interest in psychoanalysis among other Marxists. For, if the production of ideology is not the work of any identifiable group, it must be located elsewhere. Rejecting the notion of "false consciousness," many Marxists have turned to a study of the unconscious, as it is structured in and by the family. This emphasis has the merit of beginning to explain why people cling to oppressive conditions even after it is pointed out to them that their own best interests lie elsewhere. It helps explain, for example, why the sales of Harlequin Romances have not simply remained steady in recent years but have actually increased along with the growth of feminism. Only by taking psychoanalytic insights into account, by understanding how deep-rooted are the anxieties and fantasies contained in (and by) popular narratives for women can we begin to explain why women are still requiring what Jameson calls the "symbolic satisfactions" of the texts instead of looking for "real" satisfactions.

But this is easier said than done. Jameson can speak of "desires" and "anxieties" as if the terms were self-evident, but when they are applied to women and women's situation they become extremely problematic. Early followers of Freud tended to characterize women's desire as masochism, a masochism thought to be biologically ordained, for, according to Helene Deutsch, if women did not "naturally" love pain they would neither consent to sexual intercourse nor suffer the difficulties of childbearing.[39] In a classic Freudian psychological manoeuvre, women's very anxieties about pain which they revealed, for instance, in nightmares about rape, were construed by Deutsch as "proof" of women's repressed wish to be physically overpowered. We may smile at the doctrine of women's masochism when it is thus baldly stated, but it survives in milder forms to this day, and is implicitly invoked even by feminist critics when they try to explain the attractions of popular feminine

29

texts. Here is how Ann Douglas describes the Harlequin readers: "[The] women who couldn't thrill to male nudity in *Playgirl* are enjoying the titillation of seeing themselves, not necessarily as they are, but as some men would like to see them: illogical, innocent, magnetized by male sexuality and brutality."[40] It is an important part of my project to show that the so-called masochism pervading these texts is a "cover" for anxieties, desires and wishes which if openly expressed would challenge the psychological and social order of things. For that very reason, of course, they must be kept hidden; the texts, after arousing them, must, in Jameson's formula, work to neutralize them.

When applied carefully, then, a psychoanalytic approach to mass cultural texts can have some of the same value Herbert Marcuse claimed for high art and for psychoanalysis itself. In *Eros and Civilization* Marcuse argues that Freudianism contains a hidden, liberating tendency because it encourages people to explore the sources of their repression and to discover in their dreams and fantasies the long-hidden wishes which ultimately constitute a critique of repressive civilization.[41] In this sense, psychoanalysis by looking backward enables us to look forward in imagination to a "utopian" world. It is important not to overlook the utopian component of *mass* dreams and fantasies, as Jameson, Hans Magnus Enzensberger, and others have recently pointed out.[42] The Frankfurt School strenuously denied this component, insisting that only "great" art could give us foreshadowings of a better world to come. As Herbert Marcuse, waxing poetical, puts it:

> There is no work of art which does not, in its very structure, evoke the words, the images, the music of another reality, of another order repelled by the existing one and yet alive in memory and anticipation, alive in what happens to men and women, and in their rebellion against it.[43]

But Jameson accurately notes that precisely in order to legitimatize the status quo, the works of mass culture must "deflect . . . the deepest and most fundamental hopes . . . of the collectivity to which they can therefore . . . be found to have given voice."[44] To commit ourselves to a search for the utopian promises of mass art for women, or as I put it in the final chapter, to a "search for tomorrow," is to put ourselves in the way of answering the great vexed question of psychoanalysis first posed by Freud: "What do women want?"

Freud himself did not spend a whole lot of time trying to answer the question, although feminists are beginning to realize that what he did have to say about feminine psychology is of enormous interest and significance.[45] Many recent studies of psychoanalysis and women have expanded Freud's ideas most fruitfully. This work forces us to reconsider some of the generally accepted notions about psychoanalysis and literature. For if, as Freud admitted, the female's psychic development does not parallel the male's then obviously studies of literature based upon masculine psychology will prove inadequate to an understanding of "the dynamics of feminine literary response." When Norman Holland in *The Dynamics of Literary Response* discusses the psychology of the reader, he actually means the *male* reader. And Freud himself was an offender in this respect, as a look at his discussion of the uncanny sensation in literature clearly shows.[46] Freud posits fear of castration as one of the main sources of this sensation. Now, clearly women cannot have the same dread of castration that men do. In Freud's view, women, upon becoming aware that they lack a penis, accept their "castration" as a fait accompli; rather than fearing for the fate of the penis, women at most suffer feelings of inadequacy because of the male's superior penis. If this is so, it would follow that the sensation of the uncanny would be less powerful in women than in men (just as Freud, following similar logic, concluded that the superego is less developed in women[47]). But, as we shall see, Gothic novels for women continually exploit the sensation of the uncanny as it was defined by Freud to a far greater extent than any other type of mass fiction and hence point to the weakness of the classic psychoanalytic model.

I see my work in part as an early contribution to a psychology of the interaction between feminine readers and texts. Analyzing Harlequins, Gothics, and soap operas seems a good way to begin: first, because the works are aimed predominantly or exclusively at a female audience; and secondly, because these fantasies, as complex as we shall find them to be, do not employ as elaborately as "high" art the psychological and formal devices for distancing and transforming the anxieties and wishes of their readers.

IV

To this end—the end of determining what constitutes narrative pleasure for women—each of the following chapters has a different emphasis. While the three forms under consideration are by no means entirely dissimilar, each seems to satisfy particular psychological needs, and each is importantly different from the others in its narrative form.

I will begin my investigation by studying the oldest type of women's narrative, the romance, which is also the most rigid of the three forms in terms of its narrative structure. In 1793, Susanna Rowson, a writer of the "sentimental novel," remarked, "I wonder that the novel readers are not tired of reading one story so many times, with only the variation of its being told different ways."[48] While Rowson's observation could, with even more justice today, be applied to most popular novels, which are, of course, deeply conventional, it pertains most forcibly to Harlequin Romances, for the company which produces them requires its writers to follow a strict set of rules and even dictates the point of view from which the narrative must be told. The peculiar result is that the reader who reads the story *already knows the story*, at least in all its essentials. I will show that this situation both reflects and contributes to a mild "hysterical" state—using this term in its strict psychoanalytic sense. In his famous case study of Anna O., Josef Breuer, who, with Freud, worked with female hysterics, discusses the way the patient's early "habit of daydreaming" to escape from her "monotonous family life" prepared the way for the extreme hysteria she was to develop.[49] Eventually, she began to experience a kind of "double conscience," as Breuer calls it, which, among other symptoms, was manifested in a need to tell stories about herself in the third person and in a feeling that even when she was at her most "insane," "a clear-sighted and calm observer sat . . . in a corner of her brain and looked on at all the mad business."[50] This kind of duality exists, as we shall see, at the very core of romances, particularly in the relation between an "informed" reader and a necessarily innocent heroine.

Another characteristic of Anna O.'s hysteria consisted of her reliving in the present experiences which had happened in the past. Harlequins too involve the reader in regressive fantasies—both angry fantasies and fantasies of being wholly protected and cherished. But the flight into the past is perhaps most marked in the

Gothic text, in which the reader is drawn into a kind of "family romance," as the heroine, on the brink of marriage, confronts early "separation anxieties" and "oedipal difficulties." I said earlier that Roland Barthes and his many followers consider classical narrative to be based on the male oedipal drama; what I want to demonstrate in the chapter on Gothics is that there is at least one kind of story which closely follows the *female* oedipal drama. For this reason I rely more exclusively on a psychoanalytic approach in this chapter than in either of the others. We shall see that the phobias and persecution fears contained within the texts are crucially bound up with "normal" feminine psychological development. Thus, if Harlequin Romance may be called the "hysterical text," we could perhaps think of the Gothic as the "paranoid text."

Despite the significant differences, however, both texts share in common a sense of the insufficiency of female selfhood. The reader of Harlequin Romances finds herself, in "hysterical" fashion, desiring the subversion of the heroine's attempts at self-assertion; and the reader of Gothics identifies with a heroine who fears hereditary madness or who feels literally possessed by the spirits of other women from out of the past. However, feminine selflessness reaches its extreme in the "family romances" of soap operas. And this not so much because the women portrayed on these programs embody it as an ideal; rather, because of the special narrative form of soap operas (because it has no end, because, properly speaking, it has no center), the spectator is invited to disperse herself into a variety of situations which never come to a full and satisfactory conclusion. The spectator becomes the ideal woman, emptied of self, preoccupied by the perennial problems of "all her children." Moreover, in directing the spectator's hostility towards the one woman who repeatedly tries to gain control over feminine power-lessness, soap operas further insure against the possibility of women's becoming more self-assertive. The "villainess" often figures largely as a character in Harlequins and Gothics too, but I postpone a full discussion of her character until the last chapter because the emotional energy the audience invests in it appears to be most extreme in soap operas. This emotion cannot be defined as one of simple loathing, however; it consists of a complex mixture of anger, envy, and sneaking admiration.

Current film theory, even feminist film theory, assumes that the addressee of narrative film is necessarily male; indeed, this is the explicit point of Laura Mulvey's extremely influential essay,

"Visual Pleasure and Narrative Cinema," in which she argues that the spectacle and the story work together in order to stimulate masculine pleasure and alleviate basic masculine psychological insecurities. But soap operas are one visual, narrative art uniquely adapted to the psychology of the woman in the home. As we shall see, it can even be said that soap operas train women to become, like women in the home, "ideal readers"—not of texts but of people. The necessity of "reading" people, especially men, is tacitly acknowledged in the other two types of narratives as well. In both Harlequins and Gothics, the heroines engage in a continual deciphering of the motives for the hero's behavior. The Harlequin heroine probes for the secret underlying the masculine enigma, while the reader outwits the heroine in coming up with the "correct" interpretation of the puzzling actions and attitudes of the man. In Gothics the heroine, in the classic paranoid manner, broods over the slightest fluctuation in the hero's emotional temperature or facial expression, quick to detect in these alterations possible threats to her very life. Carolyn Heilbrun remarks that in popular literature, in the literary classroom, and in life, women have always had to "read" men, and she notes with irony that the only time men "read" women is "in the world of commerce," where "publishers have spent fortunes analyzing what women want, trying to discover those elements in a romance necessary to move the books fast off the shelf of the supermarket." She concludes "that women may be 'read,' their responses deciphered, only if the process reinforces woman's role as consumer, consoler, conquest."[51] It is time to begin a feminist reading of women's reading, for it is possible that even those men whose livelihood depends on deciphering women's responses have remained largely ignorant of the "evils" lurking behind the most orthodox plots. The price women pay for their popular entertainment is high, but they may still be getting more than anyone bargained for.

II

The Disappearing Act: Harlequin Romances

I

The success of Harlequin Enterprises, Ltd., which is based in Toronto, has been extraordinary.[1] Since 1958 when the first Harlequin Romance was published, over 2,300 titles have appeared. In 1977, Harlequin had 10 percent of the paperback market in North America, selling 100 million books on this continent and 50 million more in countries like Israel, Germany, and Holland. Although the United States is the chief market for Harlequins, the novels are now translated into sixteen languages.[2] Approximately 140 women write for the company, most of them British. The readership is, apparently, entirely female and comprised of women of all ages.

Twelve new books appear each month, "all displayed on standardized racks in bookstores, supermarkets, drugstores, as well as chains like Woolworth. The series is backed by heavy TV ads that push the romances, not single titles—spreading costs over a series."[3] As a result of this method of advertising, the company can sell its books more cheaply than other paperback companies ($1.00 to $1.50) and achieve a very low return factor: every novel becomes a best seller. Advertising and promotional gimmicks (such as putting Harlequins in boxes of detergent) account for part of Harlequin's success. But as Russell Nye points out, "It must be remembered that 98 percent of all books published each year are *not* best sellers, despite advertising budgets, and that if there is anything a publisher would like to know, it is why they are not."[4] Clearly, the incredible popularity of Harlequin novels indicates a degree of responsiveness in women that requires further analysis.

The publishers offer the following guidelines to prospective authors:

Harlequins are well-plotted, strong romances with a

happy ending. They are told from the heroine's point of view and in the third person. There may be elements of mystery or adventure but these must be subordinate to the romance. The books are contemporary and settings can be anywhere in the world as long as they are authentic.[5]

Each book averages approximately 187 pages, and the formula rarely varies: a young, inexperienced, poor to moderately well-to-do woman encounters and becomes involved with a handsome, strong, experienced, wealthy man, older than herself by ten to fifteen years. The heroine is confused by the hero's behavior since, though he is obviously interested in her, he is mocking, cynical, contemptuous, often hostile, and even somewhat brutal. By the end, however, all misunderstandings are cleared away, and the hero reveals his love for the heroine, who reciprocates.[6]

This formula is, of course, as old as the novel itself. Samuel Richardson's *Pamela*, about a servant girl who marries her master is, as many critics have observed, the "mother" of popular romances for women.[7] Elements of Charlotte Brontë's *Jane Eyre* can also be found in modern romances, although, as I will try to show, critics have probably overestimated the amount of female fantasy in the novel and underestimated the extent to which Brontë's novel attempts to undercut the fantasy. Finally, it has not been sufficiently recognized how much Jane Austen's *Pride and Prejudice* has contributed to the development of the formula. While there is no denying Austen's genius, we will see how she hit upon a perfect method of presenting feminine fantasy under the guise of "realism."

A television commercial for Harlequin Romances shows a middle-aged woman lying on her bed holding a Harlequin novel and preparing to begin what she calls her "disappearing act." I can't think of a better phrase to describe at once both what is laudable and what is deplorable in the appeal of such fiction. In one sense, of course—and this is the aspect critics of popular romances have spent most energy discussing— women should stop vanishing quietly behind the scenes and start making themselves more visible. This is unlikely to happen so long as they continue to feel the need to "escape" into what the commercials call "the wonderful world of Harlequin Romances." For this world, very like the real one, insists upon and rewards feminine selflessness. Indeed, as we shall see, the heroine of the novels can achieve happiness only by undergoing a complex process of self-subversion, during which she sacrifices her aggressive instincts, her "pride," and—nearly—her life. And a close analysis of the dynamics of the reading process will show that the reader is encouraged to participate in and actively desire feminine self-betrayal.

In quite another sense, however, women's longing to "disappear," their desire to obliterate the consciousness of the self as a physical presence—increasingly difficult to do these days when mass culture has turned women into delectable sights for consumption—surely cannot be completely condemned. In *Ways of Seeing*, John Berger, Marxist art critic, screenwriter, and novelist, has discussed the way in which the display of women in the visual arts and publicity images results in

> a woman's self being split into two. A woman must continually watch herself. She is almost continually accompanied by her own image of herself. Whilst she is walking across a room or whilst she is weeping at the death of her father, she can scarcely avoid envisaging herself walking or weeping. From earliest childhood she has been taught and persuaded to survey herself continually.[8]

As we shall see, romances help readers, if only temporarily, to believe in the possibility of transcending the divided self so accurately described by Berger. Moreover, they help to convince women that the price of being taken care of does not have to be eternal vigilance; all women do not have to be like Jane Eyre who, because of the inequalities between her and Rochester, was unable to relax with him, forced to "tease" rather than "please" him, forced to keep him "excellently entertained" for fear he would tire of her. According to popular romances, it is possible really to be taken care of and to achieve that state of self-transcendence and self-forgetfulness promised by the ideology of love.

The complexity of women's responses to romances has not been sufficiently acknowledged. Instead of exploring the possibility that romances, while serving to keep women in their place, may at the same time be concerned with real female problems, analysts of women's romances have generally seen the fantasy embodied in romantic fiction either as evidence of female "masochism" or as a simple reflection of the dominant masculine ideology. For instance, Germaine Greer, referring to the idealized males of women's popular novels, says, "This is the hero that women have chosen for themselves. The traits invented for him have been invented by women cherishing the chains of their bondage."[9] But this places too much blame on women, and assumes a freedom of choice which is not often in evidence—not in their lives and therefore certainly not in their popular arts.

Susan Brownmiller, on the other hand, denies women any share in the creation of their fantasies:

> Given the pervasive male ideology of rape (the mass psychology of the conqueror) a mirror-image female victim psychology (the mass psychology of the conquered) could not help but arise. Near its extreme, this female psycho-sexuality indulges in the fantasy of rape. Stated another way, when women do fantasize about sex, the fantasies are usually the product of male conditioning and cannot be otherwise.[10]

While there is a great deal of truth in these remarks, Brownmiller's "reflection theory" of female fantasies is belied by the obvious male bafflement at female romantic expectations. As Greer's witty sketch of the adolescent "courting situation" shows, female desires, shaped by romantic fiction, are very much at odds with male ones; therefore, it would seem, "female victim psychology" cannot be classified as a simple "mirror-image" of the male ideology of rape.[11] My analysis proceeds from the belief that the truth lies somewhere between the positions taken by Greer and Brownmiller. Psychologist Clara M. Thompson described women's "masochism" as a "form of adaptation to an unsatisfactory and circumscribed life."[12] The notion of "adaptation" is an important one, for it implies some sort of activity on the part of women, not just passive acceptance. In exploring female romantic fantasies, I want to look at the varied and complex strategies women use to adapt to circumscribed lives and to convince themselves that limitations are really opportunities.

In order to account for the appeal of the rigid formula, it is useful to see in each Harlequin two basic enigmas: the first, which is more or less explicitly stated (and often constantly repeated), has to do with the puzzling behavior of the hero: why does he constantly mock the heroine? Why is he so often angry at her? The second enigma, usually but not always implicit, concerns how the hero will come to see that the heroine is different from all other women, that she is not, in other words, a "scheming little adventuress." The two enigmas must necessarily be considered separately here, but it should be kept in mind that the narrative's peculiar power lies in its ability to solve them simultaneously.[13]

II

ENIGMA I: *"Who are you?" she whispered, staring up at him, her pale fingers suddenly clutching his arm as if trying to convey that the question was important to her. Beneath the thin material of his shirt she could feel the hard muscles flexing, and a tremor shot through her. She couldn't remember whether he was friend or foe. He didn't appear to be either.*[14]

In a perceptive article on Gothic novels for women, Joanna Russ claims that Gothics are written for women who are afraid of their husbands. She quotes an ex-editor of Gothics who is very frank about this point:

> The basic appeal . . . is to women who marry guys and then begin to discover that their husbands are strangers . . . so there's a simultaneous attraction/repulsion, love/fear going on. Most of the "pure" Gothics tend to have a handsome, magnetic suitor or husband who may or may not be a lunatic and/or murderer.[15]

The basic premise of these "mystery" stories is that a good man is hard to detect; the solution usually involves the discovery that the man who had seemed most suspicious and unreliable is the real hero who has been in love with the heroine all along, and the man who had seemed above suspicion—"a man invariably represented as gentle, protective, responsible, quiet, humorous, tender, and calm"—is the villain who may even be revealed "as an insane mass-murderer of a whole string of previous wives."[16]

I suggest that the mystery of masculine motives is not peculiar to Gothic novels, but is central to most women's popular romances. Although the hero of Harlequins is not suspected of being insane or murderous, he *is* more or less brutal, and it is the function of the novels to explain such brutality in a lover. The very titles often indicate the basic conflict: *Enemy Lover, Beloved Tyrant, Fond Deceiver,* etc.[17] And typically in the first meeting between hero and heroine, the man's indifference, contempt, or amusement is emphasized:

> But now she was wet, cold and late and had had a severe fright on top of it. To crown it all the detestable man stood over her without offering to help her to her feet. He even looked as if he were laughing. It occurred to her that she must look ridiculous, like some collapsed puppet sprawled at the side of the road (*Goblin*, 5–6).

> Even so, with her inexpertness, she bruised the fingers of one hand when they eventually achieved their object. The cry she gave was completely ignored, however, indeed she doubted if he even noticed it, and she stood with her bruised knuckles pressed to her mouth, looking at him reproachfully.
> He examined his own vehicle for damage, but omitted to do as much for hers. . . (*Chateau*, 11).

> All the while, without realizing it, she appeared to be amusing him no end. . . . His eyes licked over her, calculating, experimental, still brilliant with laughter (*Lesson*, 28).

> If he were a farmer he could be talking of some of his own livestock (*Captive*, 37).

Greer is very far from the truth in claiming that these fictional heroes have been "invented." Clearly, they are here asserting their masculine superiority in the same ways men often do in real life: they treat the woman as a joke, appraise her as an object, and give her less attention than they give their automobiles. The element of fantasy in romance lies less in the character traits of the hero than in the interpretation readers are led to make of his behavior. For, the reader, acquainted with the formula and hence in possession of what Wolfgang Iser calls "advance retrospection," is always able to interpret the hero's actions as the result of his increasingly intense love for the heroine.[18] Knowing the hero will eventually imply or state that he has loved the heroine from the beginning, the reader can attribute the hero's expressions of hostility and derision to his inability to admit, perhaps even to himself, how much the sight of the woman "sprawled at the side of the road looking like a collapsed puppet" inflames his passion and rouses his admiration. Male brutality comes to be seen as a manifestation not of contempt, but of love.

This is an important function of the formula. It is easy to assume, and most popular culture critics have assumed, a large degree of identification between reader and protagonist, but the matter is not so simple.[19] Since the reader knows the formula, she is superior in wisdom to the heroine and thus detached from her. The reader, then, achieves a very close emotional identification with the heroine partly because she is intellectually *distanced* from her and does not have to suffer the heroine's confusion. We shall see in Part II, however, that this mixture of detachment and identification creates special problems for the reader in that the heroine is virtuous only insofar as she remains ignorant and confused about the matters the reader clearly comprehends.

Since readers are prepared to understand the hero's behavior in terms of the novel's ending, some of the serious doubts women have about men can be confronted and dispelled. Many likely explanations for the contempt men show towards women, explanations which might be plausible enough in real life, come to seem like narrative snares—false clues—and the reader can enjoy outwitting the heroine by guessing the hero's true motives:

> It was almost as if he was feeling vicious this morning (*Enemy*, 94).

> Men, in her experience, took a woman because she was convenient and a good worker far more often than because they had conceived a grand passion for her. It was enough for her if he did no more than that—of course it was enough (*Bride*, 174).

> Arrogant and ruthless, he would take anything he wanted, but it was doubtful if his own emotions could be touched very deeply (*Chateau*, 105).

> The nicest men in the world were horribly cruel. They took no great pleasure from it, it was just a part of being a male. . . (*Lesson*, 153).

There was an odd, disturbing look on his face that flicked tiny tremors down her spine, sent sharp warning signals along her nerves which she was rash enough to ignore. He enjoyed taunting and teasing, but it would mean little. Possibly the sudden spell of bad weather had stirred a devil in him. Many men looked for scapegoats when overworked (*Captive*, 54).

The "odd, disturbing" looks men are shooting at women in every other line mediate between the heroine's worries (which, from a feminist point of view, may be perfectly justified) and the reader's interpretation of the male's behavior, which is seen as resulting from his resistance to the increasing power of her charms. The vague language, then, has a precise function; more specific language would destroy the reader's complex relationship with the heroine—causing us either to identify with her too closely or to become too detached. In other words, since his look is so "odd," we don't view her persistence in blaming it on the bad weather and a bad mood as completely unwarranted, yet we can ourselves attribute it to happier causes unsuspected by the heroine.

Almost all of the possible reasons for men's mistreatment of women are suggested in one or another of the novels. They range from fairly charitable explanations: his temper really has nothing to do with me, but with the weather and the workload—an excuse which may be soothing in real life, but which, in the novels, is still very far from the heavenly truth—to explanations which posit the emotional inferiority of men—this allows women a measure of dignity and some superiority, but is hardly acceptable since their whole lives are supposed to revolve around men—to explanations which might, in another context, be considered profound. The most constant suspicion in the novels is that men are using sexuality to punish and humiliate women. "I doubt if you would be prepared for the retribution I would exact" is a favorite male line and should be interpreted as meaning he will unleash his pent up sexual desire for the heroine.

Often, punishment miraculously turns into reward: "For an instant she thought he was going to hit her and then, fearfully, realized he was going to do something very different" (*Goblin*, 130). If kissing and hitting are so "very different," one wonders how the heroine could possibly mistake one for the other, even "for an instant." The novels perpetuate ideological confusion about male sexuality and male violence, while insisting that there is no problem (they are "very different"). The rapist mentality—the intention to dominate, "humiliate and degrade," which, as Susan Brownmiller shows, is often disguised as sexual desire—is turned into its opposite—sexual desire disguised as the intention to dominate and hurt.[20] The message is the same one parents sometimes give to little girls who are singled out for mistreatment by a bully: "he really has a crush on you." This belief is of course an enormously difficult one to sustain in real life, and romantic literature performs a crucial function in assuring us that although some men may actually enjoy inflicting pain on women, there are also "bullies" whose meanness is nothing more than the overflow of their love or the measure of their resistance to our extraordinary charms.

Thus, romances to some extent "inoculate" against the major evils of sexist society. Roland Barthes identifies inoculation as one of the principle figures of contemporary myth: "One immunizes the contents of the collective imagination by means of a small inoculation of acknowledged evil; one thus protects it against the risk of a generalized subversion."[21] Although, as we have seen, Harlequin novels do not so much acknowledge evil as transform it, Barthes' insight has some validity. Men may appear moody, cynical, scornful, and bullying, but they nevertheless provide romance and excitement. Both heroine and reader are, in Barthes' words, "rid of a prejudice which costs us dearly, too dearly, which costs us too much in scruples, in revolt, in fights, and in solitude."[22]

The cost of "revolt" is what romances stress most. Since in real life women are not often able to reinterpret male hostility in such a satisfactory way, the novels must somehow provide an outlet for female resentment. In Richardson's *Pamela*, Mr. B., after realizing he wants to marry Pamela and not rape her, writes to her of the effect her letters have had upon him:

> Your Papers shall be faithfully return'd you, and I have paid so dear for my Curiosity in the Affection they have rivetted upon me for you, that you would look upon yourself amply reveng'd if you knew what they have cost me.[23]

Mr. B.'s statement reveals more about his own inability to understand love as anything but a power struggle than it does about

Pamela's feelings, for Richardson takes great pains to show that *she* is above all such unsaintly considerations. On the other hand, I intend to show that men may be correct in suspecting women of desiring to be "amply reveng'd."

The few analyses written about romances almost always mention the childish qualities of the heroine, but no one has noted the large amount of anger expressed by the child/woman, almost to the very end of the story. The heroines rebel against the male authority figure and at times wish to be able to compete with him.

> She had the feeling that if she did move away from the tree he would make her sorry that she had done so. And yet she didn't mind that quite as much as she minded having to do what he told her (*Bride*, 13).

> The big bay had given up after its brief, helpless struggle. It stood quietly, received a few pats on the rump, some encouraging words, then Boyd Ballinger dismounted, a mere nothing in his point of view, but something quite remarkable to Rosslyn, who had a certain defensiveness about her lack of skill (*Lesson*, 63).

> Lucy drew a shaky breath and controlled the cascade of tears that threatened. She found she wanted to rage and scream as well as weep. She wanted above all to insult him as deeply and hurtfully as he had insulted her (*Goblin*, 133).

The least liberty taken by the heroine is described as being performed "militantly," "defiantly," "rebelliously." But then comes the constant reminder of the impossibility of winning:

> Stung by his detestable attack, Amanda retaliated wildly, aroused beyond the limits of discretion, wanting to hurt him as he hurt her, even while realizing the futility of such an endeavor (*Captive*, 31).

If you can't lick them, you might as well love them. It means sacrificing your pride, betraying your true self:

> "I love you," she said tremulously, assailed with a treacherous longing that swept aside any vestige of

pride in the need to be held closely within the haven of
his arms (*Haven*, 187-88).

But the hero has to do his share of suffering too:

> How it burned inside me, that delay, when I wanted so
> much to have you in my arms like this—I love you more
> than life (*Today*, 186).

> I can't bear it if you don't want me as much as I want
> you (*Bride*, 183).

> [O]ne wants either to dominate you or get down on
> one's knees and grovel at your feet (*Enemy*, 158).

A great deal of our satisfaction in reading these novels comes, I
am convinced, from the elements of a revenge fantasy, from our
conviction that the woman is bringing the man to his knees and
that all the while he is being so hateful, he is internally grovelling,
grovelling, grovelling (it is not an either–or, as the "enemy lover"
of our third quotation maintains, but both–and). It is this element
of revenge which must prevent us from analyzing the novels according to the Freudian paradigm of the young girl's maturation
process. A superficial analysis indeed reveals that most romances
are concerned with girls "outgrowing" their resentment of the male,
with their learning to forego identification with him and to form instead an erotic attachment to him. But this can come about only via
a regression to an infantile fantasy. In most of the novels, the hero
finally becomes aware of the heroine's "infinite preciousness" after
she has run away, disappeared, fallen into a raging river, or otherwise shown by the threat of her annihilation how important her life
really is. This is, as I say, a childish fantasy, but, as Karen Horney
noticed, it is common to many women and it conceals a deep-
seated desire for vengeance:

> A wife who harbors suicidal thoughts because her hus-
> band does not give her all his love, time, and interest,
> will not notice how much of her own hostility, hidden
> vindictiveness, and aggression are expressed through
> her attitude. She will feel only despair because of her
> abundant "love," while at the same time she will feel
> most intensely and see most clearly the lack of love in
> her partner.[24]

45

The "disappearing act" has long been an integral part of romances. Pamela's thoughts of suicide, motivated by the hope that Mr. B. might "perhaps, shed a few Tears over the poor Corse of his persecuted Servant," are ostensibly overcome by religious scruples; but it is precisely Mr. B.'s discovery of her suicidal thoughts (and his anguish at her subsequent departure) which brings him to acknowledge how much she means to him.[25] So Richardson has it both ways—the reader can absolve Pamela of vindictive feelings, and at the same time have the satisfaction of seeing her avenged.

Unlike Richardson, Charlotte Brontë shows acute awareness of the reality contained in the fantasy: that only by "killing themselves off" can women get men's attention. Trying to keep Mr. Rochester from treating her as a plaything, Jane Eyre must suppress her own desires and turn herself into a plaything after all:

> The system thus entered on, I pursued during the whole season of Probation; and with the best success. He was kept, to be sure, rather cross and crusty; but on the whole I could see he was excellently entertained . . . .
> Yet after all, my task was not an easy one; often I would rather have pleased than teased him.[26]

Brontë can be credited with inventing many of the characters and situations of the popular romantic mythos, although, ironically, a close reading of *Jane Eyre* shows us that even as she created, she subverted them. Jane's running away after her discovery of Mrs. Rochester, for instance, does not have the effect of bringing Rochester to his knees (he has already been there); Jane flees not in order to be found, but to find herself, to achieve economic and moral independence.[27] She is running away from, rather than into the fantasy, since to stay with Rochester would mean going against the law and her own sense of right. Brontë has been blamed for "castrating" Rochester at the end when she has him maimed in a fire.[28] But "castration" generally plays no part in typical female revenge fantasies, which depend upon the man's retaining all his potency while loving and suffering desperately. He must need her in spite of all his strength, rather than because of his weakness. At most, Rochester's state reflects the sad—not triumphant—admission that a woman only achieves equality with—not dominance over—men who are crippled in some way. Since she can't hope to aspire to their level, they must somehow come down to hers.

The Harlequin heroine's "disappearing act," then, is a way of channelling the anger and frustration expressed in the novels, and it is the logical outcome of an entire process of self-subversion the heroines are forced to undergo. For even the heroine's anger is constantly turned into a way of pleasing men, of keeping them, like Rochester, "entertained." Rebellion may be futile, but it can at least be cute; women can still be "beautiful when they're angry," if not effective:

> "You don't sound sorry," said Lucy militantly, taking exception to the appraising look.
> "I mean," he explained carefully, "that I'm sorry you're so—er—jumpy."
> "Oh!" It was a squeak of rage. She whisked out of his hands.
> He was shaking with laughter (*Goblin*, 7).

On the one hand, as readers we identify with the heroine's anger and frustration. On the other hand, due to our adherence to the rules of the formula and our desire for a happy ending, a part of us wants the man to see the heroine as a pert, adorable creature rather than as a true rebel. Our conflicting emotions as readers would seem to point up a dilemma: the heroine's expression of resentment, which is the result of and only potential remedy for her belittlement, is felt to be the very means by which she encourages her own belittlement. This can only lead to self-hatred and to more anger against the man for putting her in such an impossible situation. But our awareness of these feelings is prevented because we are prepared for the termination of the process in its logical extension: the fulfillment of the fantasy of ultimate revenge through utter self-destruction.

It is crucial to understand the double-edged nature of women's revenge fantasies. As long as resentment is accompanied by self-denigration, Harlequin Romances can hardly be said to perform a liberating function. However, once it becomes clear how much of women's anger and hostility is reflected in (albeit allayed by) these seemingly simple "love stories," all notions about women "cherishing the chains of their bondage" become untenable. What Marx said of religious suffering is equally true of "romantic suffering": it is "at the same time an *expression* of real suffering and a *protest* against real suffering."[29] In both religion and romance the fantasy of death and resurrection enables people to avenge themselves on the world while appearing fatalistic about their lot.

Our discussion thus far has resulted in a complete reversal of the usual psychoanalytical approach to women's sexuality. In applying the notion of wish fulfillment to women's dreams, psychoanalysts, notably Helene Deutsch, have found evidence of women's anxieties about rape (the manifest content) and have analyzed these anxieties as concealing the *desire* to be taken by force (latent content).[30] In looking at romance fantasies, on the other hand, we have seen that the desire to be taken by force (manifest content) conceals anxiety about rape and longings for power and revenge (latent content).

III

ENIGMA II: *"Miranda," his voice was low as his hand slid under her hair, forcing her face up, "are you telling me the truth about yourself? Girls who wander as you do are not usually without some experience, but how could I ever be sure? You're young and seemingly innocent, yet how could I tell?"* (*Captive*, 71).

Male popular culture is to female popular culture as "adventurer" is to "adventuress." If heroes must deserve the former title, heroïnes must take care not to earn the latter:

> The quiet young school teacher hadn't known he was rich when she befriended the old recluse during his last illness. But his nephew, Angus, firmly believed that Tina was nothing but a scheming little adventuress (*Enemy*, back cover).

While the novels are always about a poor girl finally marrying a rich man, preferably of the nobility, they must be careful to show that the girl never set out to get him and his goods. This is of course a simple reflection of the double bind imposed upon women in real life: their most important achievement is supposed to be finding a husband; their greatest fault is attempting to do so.

How to get your heroine from loneliness and penury to

romance and riches, without making her appear to have helped herself along or even to have thought about the matter, is an old problem for novelists, a problem which has been aggravated by the harsh treatment of literary heroines by their judges, the critics. Richardson's *Pamela* is a case in point. Richardson, of course, had been extremely careful to show that Mr. B. constantly accuses Pamela of "artfulness" in order to advance his own artful plans and to fob off his guilt onto her. In *Shamela* Henry Fielding could, nevertheless, dismiss the evidence, acquit Mr. B., and indict Pamela—the exact literary equivalent of judges siding with rapists against the victims.

Jane Austen's *Pride and Prejudice*, a novel which is centered around the contradiction between economic necessity and the feminine ideal, has been more successful in eluding such outright censure. Nevertheless, Austen is not totally successful in extricating her heroine from what Ian Watt has called "the duplicities involved in the feminine role."[31] Elizabeth Bennet at first dislikes Darcy for the very character traits which result from his richness and nobility: his pride and aloofness. In Harlequin Romances, too, the heroines are usually "determined to hate" the hero for his impossible arrogance, a quality he possesses only because of his economic security—unlike the rest of us, he bows to no man. The woman's determination to hate the hero at once absolves her of mercenary motives and becomes the very means by which she obtains the hero's love, and, consequently, his fortune. Elizabeth's "playful" tone in a speech near the end of the book shows her desire to deny the truth even as she utters it—an example, perhaps, of "irony as evasion," to paraphrase Marvin Mudrick:

> The fact is that you were sick of civility, of deference, of officious attention. You were disgusted with the women who were always speaking and looking and thinking for your approbation alone. I roused and interested you, because I was so unlike *them*.[32]

(Unlike the scheming little adventuresses.) Elizabeth's feelings undergo a decisive change when she realizes that Darcy's wealth in fact constitutes much of his superiority:

> As a brother, a landlord, a master, she considered how many people's happiness were in his guardianship!—

49

> How much of pleasure or pain it was in his power to
> bestow!—How much of good or evil must be done by
> him! . . . she thought of his regard with a deeper senti-
> ment of gratitude than it had ever raised before. . . .[33]

These feudal notions, as Ellen Moers points out, were later to be rejected by Austen;[34] but they are still the staple of Harlequin
Romances, for in a society where wealth and virtue are seen as
causally connected, the woman can admire the latter and so not be
thought a scheming little adventuress in acquiring the former:

> No good either to dwell on her previous conviction that
> they hadn't a thing in common. She loved him in spite
> of that, and she had certainly come to respect him. To
> respect his concern for his employees, his kindness in
> helping the small farmers among his neighbours, who
> were less fortunate than he was.
>   Even his autocratic manner she had come to accept
> as an inevitable result of his birth and background. It no
> longer jarred on her as it had done in the beginning
> (*Sherringdon*, 101).

We are now in a position to understand why Fielding's accusations against the romantic heroine might seem warranted. The
novels inevitably convey a contradictory message which the reader
cannot possibly internalize without feeling manipulative, for we
are repeatedly shown that although it is socially, economically, and
aesthetically imperative for a woman to get a husband and his
money, she achieves these goals partly by *not wanting* them. In
order for this to work in real life, pretense and hypocrisy must be
practiced.

And there is still another reason why we might be inclined to
assent to Fielding's criticism. Since we know the heroine must wind
up with the rich, lordly man, we feel pleasure in those episodes
which further the desired and expected ending. We tend to doubt
from the beginning the heroine's avowed dislike of the hero, and,
moreover, we are pleased whenever her expressions of this aversion
have effects contrary to what she intends—that is, whenever they
excite the hero rather than alienate him. As we saw in our discussion of resentment, we consider most of the heroine's emotions as
important only insofar as they subvert themselves. No wonder that

to some readers the whole process can feel like deception and hypocrisy.

It is easy to see why the heroines must have certain character traits. For instance, they must be shown to be "prejudiced" like Elizabeth Bennet, or, in other words, self-deluded.[35] This solves a couple of problems. If a woman is chiefly deceiving *herself* about the nature of her feelings, she can't be accused of wilfully deceiving others. And, due to the uncertain state of her emotions, she can act inconsistently, thus presenting herself to the man as a charming enigma, without being suspected of deliberately trying to stir up his interest. Further, the subversion of the heroine's negative reactions to the hero can appear as a process of self-discovery and growing self-awareness, not self-betrayal.

Therefore, the heroine's extreme youthfulness must also be stressed; and this is in contrast to the "other woman" of the novels —the real scheming adventuress—who is usually around twenty-nine and thus young enough to be a threat but too old to possess the necessary innocence. A heroine must not even understand sexual desire, for knowledge entails guilt; but since she is a child and knows not what she does, she can do a lot and be excused: she can arouse the hero by her appealing looks and her "spunky" and whimsical behavior:

> Zachary shook his head from side to side. "Jenny, Jenny," he chided gently. "You confound me. Half child, half woman—you employ contrary tactics, the consequences of which you're at a loss to understand," he concluded wryly (*Haven*, 126–127).

Along with making the heroine young, the novels often place her in circumstances where she can work on the male's sexual desires and yet not be held responsible for "the consequences." One of the authors' favorite devices is to make the heroine sick, or even unconscious. That way, she can parade around in pajamas or even be stripped and changed by the hero. In *Hold Me Captive* Amanda falls from the second story of a house into a snow bank, faints, and is taken home by Jason, who, thinking she is a boy, removes her wet clothes, and is pleasantly undeceived. At the end he admits the sight aroused him:

> You had me well nigh distracted that night when you

first came to Merington, soaked with snow and rain. You were unconscious, but I thought I'd never seen anything so lovely, so desirable (*Captive*, 185).

It is hard not to laugh at this near necrophilia, but it does reveal the impossible situation of woman: to be alive and conscious is to be suspect.

Every precaution is thus taken to make us trust in the heroine's absolute innocence. We see that the woman wasn't being deceitful; she was merely young, sick, and confused ("[I] have reason to bless God," says Pamela, "who, by disabling me in my Faculties, enabled me to preserve my Innocence").[36] By the end of the novel she will have grown up into a healthy adult woman who has achieved self-knowledge. But the reader's own guilt feelings are no doubt intensified; for how, when the novels make so clear what a woman needs and should want; how, when the characters are so unambiguously marked as good or evil, can we keep reading and still believe *we* could remain confused and self-deluded (let alone young)? The novels can be said to generate their own contradictions, resolvable only temporarily, only in the process of another novel reading.

It should be obvious by now that the heroine's extraordinary innocence cannot be explained solely in terms of some sort of feminine ideal. Rather, what Harlequins are read for is the way they deal with the contradiction between the ideal situation and real life, in which women are presumed guilty (of plotting their own rapes, of scheming to get a husband) until proven otherwise. This is even less tolerable than it might at first seem, for once women are aware of being suspected, they must try to make themselves *look* innocent, and, of course, in manipulating appearances, they forfeit the very possibility of innocence. Matters are further complicated by the fact that men are always surveying and inspecting women. Harlequin heroes are constantly sizing up the heroine, who, like a woman walking past a construction site, is uncertain how to comport herself:

Laughter glittered unmistakably in his eyes and lent a suggestion of cruelty to his wide and rather sensual mouth as he looked at her, and she felt a warm flush of colour in her cheeks as she lifted her chin. It was not easy to meet the mockery in his eyes, but she held his

gaze determinedly and with far more boldness than she
felt (*Chateau*, 26).

"Men look at women. Women watch themselves being looked
at," as Berger points out in his study of the nude in art history.[37]
And, we might add, as women watch themselves they are at every
moment incurring guilt, proving themselves to be the "narcissists"
they are often accused of being. Women can be artless and demonstrate this artlessness only in the absence of men. Unfortunately,
men are the ones they have to convince. In literature this dilemma
is generally resolved by making men into eavesdroppers: Mr. B. in
the closet observing Pamela's "artless prattling"; Rochester disguised as an old woman fortune-teller prying out the secrets of
Jane's soul; Harlequin heroes in doorways, behind bushes, in near-
by rooms listening, looking, and, finally, loving.

The man-in-the-closet plot device has undoubtedly served to
aggravate women's split consciousness. As readers we are at the
same time with Pamela in her supposed isolation, and with Mr. B.
watching and judging her. We possess the guilty knowledge that
Pamela must lack; we experience a split consciousness in order to
be reassured that a whole one is possible. Ultimately, romances
help instill in women a sense of the impossibility of *ever* achieving
self-forgetfulness. When men are not around is precisely when they
should be present, when we perhaps vaguely wish for their presence, and when we watch ourselves as if they were present.

Women's longing to be swept away, so frequently expressed in
Harlequins, must be understood in light of the foregoing discussion. The heroine's extreme passivity, like her innocence, can only
be completely accounted for when we realize to what extent the
ideal of feminine passivity conflicts with the constant mental activity women must generally engage in. Recall Jane Eyre never being
able to relax in Rochester's love, but always watching herself being
watched by him so that she can keep him "excellently entertained."
Or consider the experience of Doris Lessing's Martha Quest in the
act of love-making, one of the (to men) ultimate acts of "self-
transcendence":

> She was ready to abandon herself, but he continued to
> kiss her, murmuring how beautiful she was. Then he
> smoothed her skirt up to her knee, and stroked her legs,
> saying over and over again, in a voice troubled by

something that sounded like grief, that her legs were so lovely, she was so lovely. Her drowning brain steadied, for she was being forced back to consciousness. She saw herself lying there, half-exposed on the bed; and half resentfully, half wearily, partook, as he was demanding of her, in the feast of her own beauty. . . . [S]he was conscious of every line and curve of her own body, as if she were scrutinizing it with his eyes.[38]

Compared to this, Harlequin heroines appear almost psychically healthy:

It was breathtaking. It was frightening. A radiant entity with a will and life of its own. For a brief second Rosslyn grasped at the fact that there are forces beyond one's control. She accepted it as something inexorable, against which she had no defense, not even if she possessed all the wisdom of the world. She had lost her breath and presently she would lose all sense of herself (*Lesson*, 85).

Furthermore, as Mr. B. rightly observes, you don't "forfeit your Innocence, if you are oblig'd to yield to a Force you cannot withstand."[39]

But in order to convince the reader that self-forgetfulness can be achieved at the same time that male desires are being met, the novels once again force the unwanted self-consciousness onto the reader. To understand how this works, we need to examine the narrative point of view. The epistolary form of the novel, used by Richardson, made it impossible to show simultaneously the effect of Pamela's charms on Mr. B. and Pamela's ignorance of those charms. For Pamela herself had to tell us what Mr. B. had been seeing from the closet. Fielding's suspicion of Pamela, then, is understandable because in order to tell her own story, she came to possess the very knowledge she should never have acquired. The third person point of view, which the Harlequin Publishers require writers to use, appears to eliminate this problem. The prohibition against first person narration is therefore comprehensible, even though most of the writing is what Roland Barthes has called personal narration:

. . . some narratives, or at least some episodes can very
well be written in the third person, although their real
stance is nevertheless the first person. How are we to
decide? All one has to do is to rewrite the narrative (or
the passage) from the *he* to the *I*: as long as this operation does not entail any alteration of the discourse other
than the change of grammatical pronouns, we can be
certain that we are still in a person system.[40]

One of Barthes's commentators gives the following examples: "'he
entered a tobacco shop' can be rewritten as 'I entered a tobacco
shop', whereas 'he seemed pleased at the distinguished air his
uniform gave him' becomes an incongruous 'I seemed pleased at the
distinguished air my uniform gave me', which implies a schizophrenic narrator."[41] Now when we apply these concepts to Harlequins, they make a great deal of sense. Most of the writing is "personal," third person. As hardly any critical distance is established
between reader and protagonist, and few doubts about the
heroine's thoughts and feelings are introduced, women can freely
view the fantasy as their fantasy. The novel becomes an expression
of their own hopes and fears. But generally the third person must
be used, for at certain points the writing necessarily becomes "apersonal," precisely those points at which the woman's appearance is
noted:

> He lifted her, sweeping her up in his arms and carrying
> her out through the door, up the wide staircase to his
> room. She had never been here before. He threw her
> down on the bed and she felt herself pinned beneath the
> weight of his heavy body. She had no idea how lovely
> she looked with her hair loosened and dishevelled, her
> tremulous lips, the high flush on her soft white skin. She
> heard Jason's breath drawn sharply above the thudding
> beat of her heart. And then his lips were on hers again,
> his hands sliding to the warm skin on her back, up and
> around. She was lost, submerged, floating in a world
> where time ceased to count (*Captive*, 174–75).

Here we are, back in the closet. We can't say, "I had no idea
how lovely I looked," without implying a "schizophrenic nar-

rator." But, since almost all of the writing is meant to draw us into the fantasy, since almost all of it lends itself to rewriting (to substitution of the "I"), we can't help but incorporate to some extent these occasional "apersonal" moments into our experience of the fantasy. The reader herself becomes the "schizophrenic," in the sense excellently described by Berger: "The surveyor of woman in herself is male: the surveyed female. Thus she turns into an object —and most particularly an object of vision: a sight."[42] The problem is actually one that has long been intuitively recognized. For instance, much of the humor in the early satires of women's novels— like Austen's youthful work *Love and Freindship*—arises from the simple substitution of the "I," for we then see how readers' identification with the heroine turns feminine virtues into their opposites: innocence becomes guile; selflessness becomes insensitivity and self-absorption. The disappearing act, then, may be a temporary success, but it is an ultimate failure. In the end, women readers reemerge feeling more visible—and hence more guilty—than ever.

IV

Many of the concepts we have had recourse to in explaining romances fit neatly into Berger's two categories of the feminine consciousness:

Surveyor	Surveyed
Intellectual distance, detachment	Emotional identification
Reader's superior knowledge due to formula	Heroine's necessary ignorance
Reader's mental activity (reading & observing)	Passivity & self forgetfulness of the heroine
Impersonal narration	Personal narration

Our analysis of Harlequin romances yields fresh insight into some Freudian concepts popular culture critics routinely apply to formula literature. The theory of repetition compulsion—"the idea that art derives from some persistently disturbing psychic conflict, which, failing of resolution in life, seeks it in the symbolic form of fantasy"—has often been invoked to explain readers' addiction to formula literature.[43] We have seen that Harlequins, in presenting a heroine who has escaped psychic conflicts, inevitably increase the reader's own psychic conflicts, thus creating an even greater dependency on the literature. This lends credence to the other commonly accepted theory of popular art as narcotic. As medical researchers are now discovering, certain tranquilizers taken to relieve anxiety are, though temporarily helpful, ultimately anxiety-producing. The user must constantly increase the dosage of the drug in order to alleviate problems aggravated by the drug itself.

Our analysis also provides insight into the reasons why the "hysterical character" in our society is more often feminine than masculine. In an essay on femininity and hysteria, Howard M. Wolowitz describes the hysteric as one involved in a process which "leads further and further away from the self becoming the basis for gratification and experience into a sense of emptiness, experiential deficiency and a wish to regress back into the dependency of early childhood as a haven."[44] A typical patient explains her way of relating to the self:

> [She] realized that she constantly saw what was happening to her while it was happening, as if it were a passage in a novel that both she and others were reading, thus guaranteeing not only an audience, but one whose stereotypic, prescribed responses could be utilized as a guide to feeling her own reaction.[45]

It is easy to see that romances not only reflect the "hysterical" state, but actually, to some extent, induce it.

But it would be pointless to end with a resounding denunciation of popular novels and their readers—a conclusion encountered all too often in studies of popular fiction. An understanding of Harlequin Romances should lead one less to condemn the novels than the conditions which have made them necessary. Even though the novels can be said to intensify female tensions and conflicts, on balance the contradictions in women's lives are more responsible for the existence of Harlequins than Harlequins are for the contradictions. Wolowitz ends his study of the hysterical character by pointing out that the "psychodynamics of the hysteric are uncomfortably close to the dynamics of the idealized normal feminine personality."[46] And if, on the one hand, the novels actually contribute to women's problems, on the other hand, a study of the romances shows cause for optimism. It is no mean feat for a grown woman to make herself disappear. As Freud frequently noted, an enormous amount of psychic energy is expended when an individual strives to attain a passive state. The reader of romances, contrary to the arguments of many popular literature critics, is engaged in an intensely active psychological process. The energy women now use to belittle and defeat themselves can be rechannelled into efforts to grow and to explore ways of affirming and asserting the self. Moreover, the very fact that the novels must go to such extremes to neutralize women's anger and to make masculine hostility bearable testifies to the depths of women's discontent. Each novel, as we saw, is as much a protest against as an endorsement of the feminine condition. Finally, not all the female longings and desires expressed in Harlequins are regressive. Indeed, many of the contradictions I have discussed in this chapter derive from the attempt to adapt what for women are utopian ideals to existing circumstances. The desire to perform a disappearing act suggests women's suppressed wish to stop being seen in the old ways and to begin looking at their lives in ways that are perhaps yet to be envisioned.

III

The Female Uncanny:
Gothic Novels for Women

I

Unlike Harlequins, popular Gothic novels are not restricted to one publisher, but are sold by a number of large publishers such as Ace and Fawcett. As a result, the Gothic formula is not quite as rigid as the Harlequin formula. The term "Gothic" is often used loosely to designate "suspense." Thus, Gothics tend to shade off, on the one hand, into the classical detective story and, on the other hand, into something like a Harlequin Romance which contains a little mystery thrown in for added spice. We will be concerned with neither of these, but with what the ex-editor of Ace Books calls "'pure' Gothics."[1]

Gothics can be identified by their cover illustrations: each portrays a young girl wearing a long, flowing gown and standing in front of a large, menacing-looking castle or mansion. The atmosphere is dark and stormy, and the ethereal young girl appears to be frightened. In the typical Gothic plot, the heroine comes to a mysterious house, perhaps as a bride, perhaps in another capacity, and either starts to mistrust her husband or else finds herself in love with a mysterious man who appears to be some kind of criminal. She may suspect him of having killed his first wife (one recalls Catherine Morland's suspicions of General Tilney in Jane Austen's *Northanger Abbey*) or of being out to kill someone else, most likely herself. She tries to convince herself that her suspicions are unfounded, that, since she loves him, he must be trustworthy and that she will have failed as a woman if she does not implicitly believe in him. Often, but not always, the man is proven innocent of all wrongdoing by the end of the novel, and the real culprit is discovered and punished.

A casual reader might at first suppose that the romantic formula and the Gothic formula are very similar. Indeed, even Kathryn

Weibel, a student of women's popular culture, claims that the differences between the two types of stories are "so minor . . . that they might not seem worth mentioning fifty years hence."[2] I have already had occasion to note some of the similarities between Gothics and Harlequins. Both deal with women's fears of and confusion about masculine behavior in a world in which men learn to devalue women. Harlequins enable women to believe that devaluation is only apparent, a mask, as it were, hiding the man's intense and ferocious love for the woman. But immediately we encounter some striking differences between the two types of narratives. In Gothic novels, the woman often suspects her lover or her husband of trying to drive her insane, or trying to murder her or both. Clearly, even the most disturbed reader would have difficulty attributing this bizarre behavior on the part of the male to a suppressed though nearly uncontrollable passion for the heroine. Another way of expressing the difference between the two types of narrative is to say that the Harlequin heroine's feelings undergo a transformation from fear into love, whereas for the Gothic heroine, the transformation is from love into fear:

> That was the point at which I knew that love had gone out of my marriage, but not the point at which fear replaced it.[3]

> She stared blindly down at his fingers, not hearing Max Alexander's voice, aware of nothing except that Jon [her husband] was a stranger to her whom she could not trust. It occurred to her dully to wonder if she had ever imagined unhappiness to be like this; it's not the raw nagging edge of desolation, she thought, but the tight darkness of fear. The pain is convex and opaque and absolute (*Shore*, 166–67).

In Harlequins, the transformation is aided by the reader's own participation in the story: she knows that the heroine has nothing to fear but love and thus she has a certain measure of power over the heroine and a feeling of being somewhat in control of the situation. In Gothics, on the other hand, the reader shares some of the heroine's uncertainty about what is going on and what the lover/husband is up to. The reader is nearly as powerless in her understanding as the heroine.

Perhaps one way of explaining the differences between the two forms of romance is to see them as corresponding to two different stages in a woman's life: roughly, courtship and marriage (the third form under consideration, soap opera, covers yet a third stage—motherhood and family life). Although this breakdown is somewhat overschematized, since studies show that a large number of college students are "hooked" on soap operas, and women of all ages tend to read romances and Gothics, it nevertheless has a certain heuristic value. It must be remembered, too, that psychologically speaking, all stages are more or less present at all times: the young woman anticipates future life; the older woman is a product of her past, or indeed reenacts the past in present relationships. In Harlequins, then, the preoccupation is with getting a man; in Gothics the concern is with understanding the relationship and the feelings involved once the union has been formed.

According to the ex-editor of Ace Books, "pure Gothics" almost always have "a handsome, magnetic suitor or husband who may or may not be a lunatic and/or murderer."[4] Immediately one is struck by the strong element of paranoia suggested by this description, an element which surely requires a deeper explanation than the one Joanna Russ assigns it:

> In one way the Gothics are a kind of justified paranoia: people *are* planning awful things about you; you *can't* trust your husband (lover, fiance); everbody's motives *are* devious and complex; only the *most* severe vigilance will enable you to snatch any happiness from the jaws of destruction.[5]

But this "justification" is what psychoanalysts who have studied the paranoid process call "the core of truth," which, they emphasize, is always present in paranoid delusions.[6] Clearly, the core of truth in Gothics is not as large as in Harlequins. As we pointed out earlier, men *are* often cynical, mocking, and hostile in their relationships with women, just as the Harlequin heroes are. But they are *not* often lunatics or murderers. Thus, while we will try never to lose sight of the "core of truth" in our discussion of Gothics, we will necessarily have to look further to discover the appeal of the story of the persecuted heroine.

At least two psychoanalysts have expressed surprise over the lack of psychoanalytic literature on paranoia in married women, since, according to these analysts, the phenomenon is not uncommon.[7] We must ask, then, why marriage causes some women to become fearful and suspicious. We will begin by examining the social circumstances which are likely to foster a paranoid attitude toward the world; and then we will examine the psychological determinants of paranoia (bearing in mind that the social and psychological are, of course, mutually determining).

Norman Cameron, one of the foremost experts on paranoia, has cited social isolation as a major contributing factor to paranoia:

> Isolation leaves a person at the mercy of his private daydreams without the safeguard of countervailing external contacts, without the corrective effects that the talk and action of others normally provide. Experimental work in sensory deprivation with normal subjects, and recent extensive studies of dreams and daydreams have brought such factors into prominence.[8]

This is hardly a new insight: one recalls Dr. Johnson's cautions against the solitary life and his portrayal of the mad astronomer, who certainly had more than a little in common with Freud's Dr. Schreber.[9] The constant stress on sociality one encounters in eighteenth-century literature must have arisen, in part, as a defense against the increasing isolation brought about by the formation of the nuclear family as well as the increase in the amount of leisure time that needed to be filled.

Obviously, all this has special pertinence for eighteenth-century women, who were expected as a matter of course to leave their own familiar surroundings and go wherever the husband dictated and who, according to a newly forming ideology, were supposed to be idle. Moreover, women's sense of reality, even before the extreme change brought about by marriage, must often have been somewhat tenuous. As Mary Wollstonecraft complained in her Gothic novel, *Maria, or the Wrongs of Woman,* young girls' lives were all too often cramped and confined. Cameron informs us that among the early social causes of the development of paranoid behavior are lack of "freedom to explore the neighborhood at an early age and [little] cooperative play with other children."[10] One can readily understand why women were ripe candidates for novels expressing delusions of persecution—as well as why for Jane

Austen's Catherine Morland, Gothic delusions were only a temporary aberration from which she easily recovered:

> She was moreover noisy and wild, hated confinement and cleanliness, and loved nothing so well in the world as rolling down the slope at the back of the house. . . . [I]t was not very wonderful that Catherine, who had by nature nothing heroic about her, should prefer cricket, base ball, riding on horseback, and running about the country, to books. . . .[11]

It can scarcely be an accident, then, that the female Gothic arose in the latter part of the eighteenth century. Indeed, one of Ann Radcliffe's explicit purposes in *The Mysteries of Udolpho*, the prototype of the female Gothic, was to warn women against indulging in paranoid fancies and to exort them to keep busy in their solitude, the breeding ground for such fancies. Over and over again, Emily St. Aubert's superstitious fears are quieted as they are shown to have quite reasonable explanations:

> 'I perceive' said Emily, smiling, 'that all old mansions are haunted; I am lately come from a place of wonders; but unluckily, since I left it, I have heard almost all of them explained.'[12]

But the explanations are notoriously unsatisfactory. Critics from Coleridge to the present have expressed irritation and frustration at the simple and mundane solutions Radcliffe gives to the most elaborate plots.[13] In their book on *The Paranoid*, Swanson et al. note that "paradoxically, [the paranoid] will often suspect complicated motives behind the simplest acts or will supply surprisingly simple, naive explanations for situations that are very complicated."[14] Perhaps Radcliffe's own social isolation rendered her incapable of dealing with the full complexity of events, forcing her to the paranoid extremes of making much out of very little, or, conversely, of minimizing the frightening atrocities to which her imagination continually led. The result is that one's own paranoid tendencies are somewhat intensified by a reading of the *Mysteries*, since we are left with a strong sense that the world of human events is terrifyingly out of kilter: everything is always a great deal more or a great deal less than it seems.[15] Be that as it may, Gothics to this day perform the contradictory function of showing women that while there is some basis for their paranoid fears, they must also struggle against succumbing to them:

> As she at last put down the receiver and looked at the silent innocent shape of the telephone she wondered if she were getting a persecution complex.
>
> People with those, she had heard, were suspicious of everybody and everything. They swore things had happened that hadn't. Their mania came from a secret profound desire for love. . . . She pressed her hands to her temples as a shout rose up in her. *What is happening to me?* (*Afternoon*, 79).

The feelings of social isolation imposed upon women who are suddenly thrust into relatively unfamiliar surroundings, an environment chosen and dominated by another, go a little way toward explaining the development of slight paranoid tendencies in certain married women. Another contributing and related factor is, no doubt, the letdown women feel as their dreams of romance and marital bliss (dreams which Harlequins promise will be utterly fulfilled) inevitably conflict with harsh reality. Cameron describes how in the early phases of paranoia, the individual begins to experience "feelings of estrangement and puzzlement. . . . [T]hings have changed for him inexplicably; and he tries to understand what is happening."[16] Gothics provide one kind of outlet for women's feelings of estrangement and the sense of disorientation consequent upon what is usually considered the most momentous change in their lives. And so a frequent complaint of Gothic heroines is that environments which had in the past seemed so various and so beautiful are now menacing and ugly. Things have changed "inexplicably":

> For Harriet Delvaney, the great house of Menfreya, standing like a fortress on the Cornish coast, has always been a citadel of happiness and high spirits. Not until she comes to Menfreya as a bride does Harriet discover the secret family legend of infidelity, jealousy, and murder (*Menfreya*, back cover).[17]

Cameron goes on to describe the paranoid's reaction to these feelings of bewilderment:

He scrutinizes his surroundings uneasily, engages in solitary observations [one thinks of Jane Eyre on the window seat], and looks for hidden meanings. He watches the little things people do and say, their glances and gestures, their frowns, smiles and laughter. He listens to conversations, asks leading questions and ponders over it all like a detective.[18]

One could scarcely draw a more accurate picture of the Gothic heroine's reactions to what goes on in the novels. Thus, the "Over-Subtle Emotions," which Russ identifies as characteristic of female Gothics constitute a classic paranoid trait.[19] To Cameron, this type of behavior marks the beginnings of an attempt to reestablish contact with social reality. The individual is on her way to constructing what Cameron felicitously calls a "pseudo-community"[20] of persecutors, of which the individual, in reaction to her feelings of loneliness and neglect, becomes the important center:

Mistrust seemed to creep toward me from every corner of the room—mistrust of every person in this house. . . . I felt like an innocent fly who had wandered into a spider's web and that all around me the spiders were gathering, ready to strangle me with strands of that web (*Dragonmede*, 270).

To be persecuted, as several analysts have observed, is better than being ignored.

But surely to be loved and admired is better than being persecuted. Yet Gothics are never about women who experience delusions of grandeur and omnipotence (a form paranoia occasionally takes); the Gothic heroine always feels helpless, confused, frightened, and despised. Obviously, then, to cite romantic disillusionment and feelings of social isolation in the newly married woman is not sufficient to explain the particular kinds of fantasies encountered in female Gothics. We must look deeper into the dynamics of the paranoid process as well as into female psychology in order to see how women come to form certain kinds of attitudes toward their husbands and, consequently, how Gothics help them to understand these attitudes.

II

In his massive study on *The Paranoid Process*, William Meissner claims that the paranoid usually comes from a family whose power structure is greatly skewed: one of the parents is perceived as omnipotent and domineering, while the other is perceived (and most usually perceives him/herself) as submissive to and victimized by the stronger partner. According to Meissner, the paranoid patient tends to introject these images of his/her parents and, even more importantly, internalizes the dynamics of the parental interaction: thus, the patient enacts within the self the war between victim and victimizer. When the internal battle becomes too painful to be tolerated, one of these elements gets projected onto the external environment—usually the aggressive introject, for, as Meissner points out, "aggressive impulses are tolerated best and with least conflict when we believe we are the victims of another's hostility."[21] It should be clear how this has special relevance for the situation of women, since aggressive impulses are socially less acceptable in women than in men. Furthermore, since an imbalance in the power structure—with the male dominant— is considered the ideal familial situation in our culture, and since the aim of our socialization process is to get the child to identify with the parent of the same sex, the female is more likely than the male to retain the (feminine) "victim" introject and to deny (project) feelings of aggression and anger. At this point, we can see how Gothics, like Harlequins, perform the function of giving expression to women's hostility towards men while simultaneously allowing them to repudiate it. Because the male appears to be the outrageous persecutor, the reader can allow herself a measure of anger against him; yet at the same time she can identify with a heroine who is entirely without malice and innocent of any wrongdoing.

But both the paranoid process and Gothic novels are even more complex than this description suggests. The child, according to Meissner, not only feels anger at the domineering father, but also at the mother for allowing herself to be a victim and for—as often happens—taking out her own anger and aggressive impulses on the helpless child. And, in addition to harboring hostile feelings toward the parents, the child must contend with its love for and great dependence on both of the parents. To Meissner, then, the paranoid "cure" consists in the patient's being able to work through many of these ambivalent emotions.[22] I suggest that Gothics provide one way for women to come at least partially to terms with their ambivalent attitudes towards the significant people in their lives.

Indeed, this was an important function of the earliest female Gothic, *The Mysteries of Udolpho*. Ellen Moers has suggested that in Radcliffe's novel, "the narrative as a whole is designed to accord with the rhythms of a woman's life. . . . [Radcliffe] blocks out the narrative in terms of female childhood, youth, and faded maturity.[23] I would go even further and claim that the narrative is blocked out in terms of the vicissitudes of the female's *psychic* life. We note that at the very beginning of the novel Emily St. Aubert's relationship with both her parents is a very harmonious one, a harmony which is almost immediately interrupted by the death of Emily's mother. The young girl's "oedipal" wish to have the father completely to herself is conveniently and rapidly fulfilled. But it is not long before the idyllic relation between father and daughter is severed, for M. St. Aubert himself soon dies, leaving Emily under the care of a vain, capricious and wilful aunt, Madame Cheron. In a study "On Women Who Hate Their Husbands," analyst David A. Freedman observes that as a child each of his paranoid women patients felt rejected by her father and "thrown on the mercies of a maternal figure toward whom her feelings were highly ambivalent."[24] This is clearly Emily's situation: "abandonment" by the father followed by submission to a tyrannizing mother figure:

> The love of sway was her [Madame Cheron's] ruling passion, and she knew it would be highly gratified by taking into her house a young orphan, who had no appeal from her decisions, and on whom she could exercise without controul the capricious humour of the moment.[25]

Sometime later Madame Cheron marries Montoni, who takes her and Emily off to the mysterious and threatening Castle of Udolpho in Italy. The ensuing family dynamic which is enacted between Montoni, the evil, omnipotent tyrant, and his wife, the tormented and depressive victim, also finds an echo in Freedman's study: the mothers of his patients, he reports, were all isolated, paranoid women, convinced "that this is a man's world and all men are selfish. . . . Open conflict between the parents characterized [the] homes, involving accusations leveled against the father as a selfish, exploiting tyrant."[26] The relationship between Montoni and his wife reaches its climax when he imprisons her in a turret and allows her to die from a languishing fever.

A number of interesting points arise from this description of the plot. Ellen Moers has pointed out that Montoni is the evil father, "a shattered mirror image of the impossibly good father," M. St. Aubert.[27] Yet she does not notice that Madame Montoni is in many ways the reverse image of the impossibly good mother.[28] That real mothers are often conspicuously absent in early literature by women has often been commented upon, but very little explanation for this phenomenon has been forthcoming. Patricia Meyer Spacks remarks in an interesting aside that female writers before the twentieth century deal with their anger towards their mothers by eliminating them, and there is certainly some truth in this claim.[29] But while real mothers (as compared to real fathers) are in short supply in female fiction, one encounters no lack of mother substitutes—aunts, older women friends, etc. This substitution, one might speculate, provides a means by which ambivalence towards the mother can be worked through while it simultaneously prevents the mother/daughter relationship from being confronted too openly.

Gertrude Ticho comments that for the female "the separation from home [as in marriage] revives early separation anxieties and unresolved oedipal conflicts."[30] She suggests that a woman can achieve autonomy and relinquish her "masochistic identification with her mother"—the victim who in turn victimizes the child— "only by working through her hostility and, most important, her love for her mother." And if this is not possible, "if the mother is in reality unpleasant, at least some tolerance of her difficulties should become possible."[31] Thus in the classic female Gothic, part of the heroine's progress involves a separation from home, a series of internal and/or external conflicts, and a more or less gradual understanding of the "mother's" situation. In *The Mysteries of Udolpho* Emily forgets "her resentment . . . impressed only by compassion for the piteous state of her aunt, dying without succour." She "watched over her with the most tender solicitude, no longer seeing her imperious aunt in the poor object before her, but the sister of her late beloved father, in a situation that called for all her compassion."[32] And in *Jane Eyre* even Jane's passionate hatred of Mrs. Reed is eventually overcome:

"Love me, then, or hate me, as you will," I said at last,

"you have my full and free forgiveness: ask now for
God's and be at peace."

Poor suffering woman! it was too late for her to make
now the effort to change her habitual frame of mind.
Living, she had ever hated me—dying, she must hate
me still.[33]

Modern Gothics, too, help women to deal with their ambivalent attitudes towards their mothers as well as their "masochistic
identification" with them. Thus in a great many of the novels the
heroine has the uncanny sensation that the past is repeating itself
through her. Usually she feels a strong identification with a woman
from either the remote or the very recent past, a woman who in
almost every case has died a mysterious and perhaps violent or
gruesome death. In *The Lady in the Tower* the heroine learns of the
legend of the young and beautiful woman walled up in a tower and
left to die by her husband:

I could not think of any wickedness that would merit
such a fate. I could not imagine seeing the last stones set
into place. The last of the air, hands clawing, nails
breaking, screams that only yourself could hear (*Lady*,
73).

In *Menfreya in the Morning* the heroine strongly resembles a
woman from the past who was locked into a buttress and died with
her child as she waited for her husband, the lord of the castle, to
return to her. In *Ammie, Come Home* a woman who had been
murdered by her father actually takes possession of the heroine,
who describes the sensation thus:

You know the feeling, when you're waiting for something that you know will be very painful or unhappy?
Like an operation; or somebody is going to die. Something you can't get out of, but that you know you are
going to hate. You can't breathe. You keep gasping, but
the air won't go down into your lungs. You can hear
your own heart thudding, so hard it seems to be banging
into your ribs. Your hands perspire. You want to run
away, but you can't, it won't do any good, the thing
you're afraid of will happen anyhow (*Ammie*, 87–88).

In *Spindrift* the heroine identifies with a mad woman out of the past:

> I stared at him in distress, because my own story and
> Zenia's were beginning to be intertwined. . . . I was
> trapped in my age as Zenia had been trapped in hers
> (*Spindrift*, 281–82).

And in *Monk's Court* the heroine comes across a statue of a woman reputed to have cut off her hands to ransom a husband captured in the crusades. The heroine becomes obsessed with this woman and, reflecting on their common situation, thinks:

> The somnolent world of Monk's Court; the dreamworld
> of Monk's Court, with herself trapped in the dream.
> And, as in all dreams—all nightmares—the dreamer,
> struggling to waken, struggling desperately, was help-
> less (*Monk's Court*, 122).

Joanna Russ, who notes this constant doubling in Gothics, asks, "Is it that every woman fears the same man and undergoes the same fate? Is it an echo of the family romance in which the Heroine plays daughter, the Super-Male is father, and the Other Woman/First Wife plays mother?"[34] Russ does not pursue the issues she raises, but her questions are very much to the point.

We can perhaps go even further: it is not only that women fear being *like* their mothers, sharing the same fate, but also that, in an important sense, they fear *being* their mothers—hence the emphasis on identity in physical appearance, the sensation of actually being possessed, the feeling that past and present are not merely similar but are "intertwined," etc. In each case, the heroine feels suf-focated—as well as desperate and panic stricken in her inability to break free of the past. We recall Ticho's remark that the separation from home revives early separation anxieties. As Nancy Chodorow persuasively argues, the female child generally has more difficulty than the male child in separating herself from the mother. Case studies of mother–child relationships reveal that while the mother recognizes the boy's differences from herself, she often

> does not recognize or denies the existence of the
> daughter as a separate person, and the daughter herself

then comes not to recognize, or to have difficulty recog-
nizing, herself as a separate person. She experiences herself, rather, as a continuation or extension of . . . her
mother.[35]

At one point Chodorow quotes the poet Ann Sexton, "A woman *is*
her mother/That's the main thing."[36]

The doubling of characters in Gothics recalls Freud's discussion of the uncanny in literature. Freud gives at least two possible
sources for this sensation: the fear of repetition and the fear of castration. As I noted in Chapter I, such a theory implies women's inability to experience the full power of the uncanny. But suppose we
view the threat of castration as part of a deeper fear—fear of never
developing a sense of autonomy and separateness from the mother.
After all, the boy achieves this sense of separateness largely
through becoming aware of the anatomical difference between himself and his mother. Castration is perceived to be threatening in
part because it would deny this difference. If this is true, we find an
unexpected connection between the two sources of the uncanny:
the fear of repetition—"an involuntary return" to a situation which
occurred in the past and which results in a "feeling of helplessness"[37]—and the fear of castration are two aspects of the more
primal fear of being lost in the mother. If my speculations are correct and the uncanny has its chief source in separation anxieties,
then it follows that since women have more difficulty establishing a
separate self, their sense of the uncanny may actually be stronger
than men's. Certainly I can think of no genre of male popular literature which so continually exploits the sense of the uncanny.

Gothics, then, serve in part to convince women that they are
not their mothers. This difference is usually established through the
discovery of what really happened to the victimized woman with
whom the heroine has been identified. Thus, "separation" occurs
partly as a result of developing an understanding of the "mother's"
difficulties. Once the characters in *Ammie, Come Home* have
learned Ammie's full story, she stops trying to "enter" the heroine
and is finally able to rest. In *Spindrift* and *The King of the Castle*,
the heroines both discover diaries detailing the other woman's life;
by gaining insight into her life they manage to achieve a measure of
distance from her:

The girl, innocent and ignorant, had been taught to re-

gard marriage with horror; the disillusion of them both;
she in finding a virile young husband, he a frigid wife
(*King*, 284).

There are some striking differences between the typical popular Gothic plot and the plot which Sandra Gilbert and Susan Gubar
take to be the "paradigmatic female story."[38] For Gilbert and
Gubar, this is the story of the imprisoned madwoman whose anger
and rebelliousness represents the heroine's own repressed rage and
whose forced confinement functions paradoxically both as a
metaphor for the restrictions of the feminine role and as a warning
against stepping outside this role, demanding a larger freedom. The
imprisoned woman in our stories, by contrast, is presented not as a
rebel, but almost wholly as a victim, even a self-victimizer (e.g. the
woman who cut off her own hands), and it is against assuming the
victim's role that the heroine desperately struggles. This too is an
old plot, and may be equally paradigmatic. We have seen it in the
earliest female Gothic, and it can also be seen in other popular
works written before the twentieth century.

Some of Louisa May Alcott's thrillers are variations on this
plot, with the interesting difference that the mother figure in
Alcott's stories is often a real mother rather than a substitute. In "A
Whisper in the Dark," the heroine, Sybil, is locked into an insane
asylum by a vicious and degenerate man who poses as her uncle in
order to gain possession of her fortune. There, she begins to hear
incessant footsteps in the room directly above her, and before long
Sybil is unconsciously pacing her room in time to the pacing of the
person upstairs—another instance of "possession," which reaches
its climax when the mysterious person is found dead:

> the face I saw was a pale image of my own. Sharpened
> by suffering, pallid with death, the features were as
> familiar as those I used to see; the hair, beautiful and
> blond as mine had been, streamed long over the pulse-
> less breast, and on the hand, still clenched in that last
> struggle, shone the likeness of a ring I wore, a ring be-
> queathed me by my father. An awesome fancy that it
> was myself assailed me: I had plotted death and with the
> waywardness of a shattered mind, I recalled legends of
> spirits returning to behold the bodies they had left.[39]

Of course, the woman turns out to have been Sybil's mother. Sybil is able to effect her escape shortly after finding a letter from the woman, a letter assuring her, "I try to help you in my poor way"; describing the mother's love for her child, "I sing to lull the baby whom I never saw"; and urging the young woman to get away before she too becomes helplessly, hopelessly mad, "for the air is poison, the solitude fatal."[40] Thus Sybil is assured that her mother has not voluntarily "abandoned" her, that on the contrary, she has done all in her meager powers to help the daughter achieve the freedom the mother has been denied. Sybil, then, achieves autonomy because love for the mother and "tolerance" for her "difficulties" has indeed become possible.

III

Thus far we have been analyzing Gothics in terms of the separation anxieties which, as Ticho observes, the female often relives upon leaving home. According to Ticho, we remember, unresolved oedipal conflicts are also experienced at this time. Separation anxieties and oedipal conflicts are of course interrelated, and for females, as many analysts have observed, the interrelationship is especially complex and the resolution of the anxieties and conflicts fraught with difficulties.[41]

For the female child, as well as for the male child, the mother is (in our society) the first and strongest attachment. Children of both sexes first perceive the father as "the enemy"—the person capable of taking the mother away from the child. We might say that from the very beginning of the child's life what we have seen to be the typical "paranoid" family dynamic is incipient in the interaction among the three family members: the child perceives the father as capable of controlling the mother and hence develops hostility towards both parents, the father because he is the "tyrant" and the mother because she is unable or unwilling to resist her husband's "control" over her. Later in the child's life, however, the father comes to be valued for the very function which was originally resented—his aid in furthering the child's necessary separation from the mother. As Chodorow remarks, children of both sexes tend to see the father as a "symbol of freedom from . . . dependence and merging."[42] The boy, as is well known, accomplishes his separation by identifying with the former "enemy"; the girl, like the boy, must relinquish her first love—her mother—but, unlike the boy, she

must make her "enemy" her "lover" (We recall the Harlequin titles).
If the father is seen to be remote and/or rejecting, the child may be
thrown back on its mother, and for several reasons the merging is
likely to be more thoroughgoing in the girl's case: because, as we
have seen, the mother perceives the female child as "an extension of
herself," because the female child does not distinguish herself from
her mother by virtue of an anatomical difference, and because,
while the boy may still "identify" with a remote father, a girl can
hardly consider herself well loved by such a parent. At this point,
the girl is likely to feel renewed hostility toward the father: he has
once again disappointed his daughter and one again becomes the
enemy.

Meissner suggests that the "need for an enemy," a classic
paranoid trait, may very well be a necessary step in the process of
separation–individuation each child must undergo, for the self
largely comes to be defined through opposition and differentia-
tion.[43] But now we encounter the knottiest problem. If the mother
perceives her husband to be an enemy—a tyrant and victimizer—
then the "enemy" father only serves to confirm rather than break
the young girl's identification with the mother. And, given the fact
that in our society men are often dominant within the home, one
would expect feelings of victimization, however slight, to be relatively common in wives and mothers (an expectation which, as we
have seen, is confirmed by Freedman's study). The mother-
daughter boundary confusion which Chodorow speaks of is, then,
aggravated both by the father's remoteness from his children and
by his powerful position in relation to his wife. According to
analysts who have studied paranoia, "confusion about the boundaries of the self, causing difficulty in locating the problem or discomfort . . . is the essence of projection."[44]

This analysis helps us to account for two strong tendencies in
Gothic novels: the desperate need of the heroine to find out who
her "enemy" is and the equally imperative desire to discover that
the enemy is *not* the father (or the lover, who is the father substitute). For, on the one hand, being able to project an enemy enables
the paranoid to establish the boundaries of the self and also, as we
have seen, allows her to deny intolerable ambivalent feelings,
especially aggressive ones ("I do not want to harm him; he is perse-
cuting *me*"). But, on the other hand, to find out that the enemy is
indeed the "father" would only increase the "boundary confusion"
the "paranoid" is struggling to eliminate.

The Gothic heroine's intense need to locate an enemy she can blame for her "discomfort" is repeatedly expressed in the typical paranoid manner described by Swanson: "Statements are frequently made about wanting to find out the real truth. Every action, every unexplained statement is scrutinized closely." The purpose of this behavior is "to find a basis for the mistrust."[45]

> It was better to bring it into the open and face it once and for all. Answers could only be found if I retraced my steps, watching for some betrayal along the way that would point to guilt. I knew there was guilt (*Spindrift*, 46).

> . . . she longed to take him in her arms and say, Jonny, why didn't you tell me about the anonymous phone call? . . . And why did you say nothing else to Marijohn and she say nothing to you? The conversation should have begun then, not ended. It was all so strange and so puzzling, and I want so much to understand. . . ."
> But she said nothing, not liking to confess that she had eavesdropped on their conversation by creeping back downstairs and listening at the closed door. . . . (*Shore*, 111–12).

Often the attempt to find an enemy and the attempt to exonerate the father are part of the same project: the heroine of *Spindrift*, for example, undertakes to prove that her father did not really kill himself, as everyone else in the novel keeps insisting, but was, in fact, murdered. Such a plot, we can speculate, serves a variety of functions. Feminine feelings of anger against the father can be simultaneously expressed and denied (the father is killed off, but the heroine's determined efforts to find out who did it help to avenge his murder). Moreover, feminine fears of abandonment by the father are assuaged (the father did not "desert" his daughter by killing himself). The plot of *Someone Waiting* is very similar: the heroine is the only person in the novel to believe that her guardian's death was a murder and not a suicide:

> Leonie soon sensed that the house was hostile to her, that someone was watching her, waiting—for she had stubbornly reopened the issue of Marcus's murder (*Waiting*, back cover).

And in *Orphan of the Shadows* the heroine sets out to prove that her father was not really a Nazi (!) as her uncle has told her all her life.

However, the most typical plot of female Gothics, as Russ observes, is one in which the lover plays the "father," and the heroine either suspects him of having killed his first wife or else fears that her own relationship with him will be a repetition of one which occurred in the past (perhaps involving one of the man's ancestors). Thus, in *Monk's Court*, the heroine believes she witnessed a murder committed by the man she loves. Throughout the novel she tries to deny the testimony of her own eyes, constantly telling herself that true love means maintaining absolute faith in the loved one. She compares her situation to that of the woman who cut off her hands to ransom her husband.

> Catharine, lying there, brave Catharine. Brave at the last, at any rate. Had she, too, flinched, and shrunk from the giving of her gift of love? . . . How deeply, deeply, she must have loved, how passionately, with both her soul and her body. Two hands gone. Two hands that had willingly, gladly been held out. How could she? Mutilation, truly the gift of gifts. More than life (210).

But though the heroine accepts the ideal of feminine self-sacrifice in theory, she can never really apply it to herself. Rather, women's fears that marriage involves either voluntary self-mutilation (as in the above quote) or involuntary victimage (the-woman-imprisoned-in-the-tower motif) must be put to rest by establishing beyond any doubt the fact that the lover/husband is not guilty:

> . . . she would stay on here, a little longer, anyway, in hope of finding proof of his innocence. It was all very well to say that true faith, faith worthy of the name, had no need of proof, but it was proof, and proof alone, that would make her existence endurable (*Monk's Court*, 179).

Only after the heroine has obtained "absolute proof" of the man's innocence can "oedipal conflicts" be resolved and reconciliation with the father become possible; only then can identification with the victimized "mother" be broken; and only then can the lover be accepted.

Moreover, in Gothics the process of detachment from the "mother" through attachment to the "father" is often overdetermined—additional proof, if it is needed, of the intensity of female "separation anxieties" and "oedipal difficulties."[46] Russ mentions the frequency with which young children appear in Gothics—their only function, apparently, to be befriended by the heroine. Russ sees this plot device simply as an easy and quick way of establishing the heroine's "goodness" and keeping her at the same time solidly within the feminine role.[47] But the child in these novels also serves as an additional reassurance that the heroine will be unlike the "mother"—a helpless, depressive victim who is therefore unable to protect the child against the tyrannies of the father or to provide it with adequate love and nurturance.[48] In each novel in which a child appears, the main male figure seems to despise it, or at the very least to be utterly indifferent towards it. In *The King of the Castle* and *The Lady in the Tower* the child is convinced its father has murdered its mother. In *Nine Coaches Waiting* the heroine believes that the man she loves is out to murder his nephew. In all cases, the heroine, who may be too timid ever to speak up for herself or to act in order to further her own claims, is able to brave the man's fiercest wrath in the interests of the child. The heroine's intervention between "father" and child is usually very effective, causing the man to show more interest in and tenderness towards the child. In *Monk's Court*, for example, the male alternates between sarcasm and indifference in his treatment of his daughter until the heroine speaks up for the girl:

> With her courage failing then, she moved quickly to the stairs, but on the first step she paused and turned, and daring the rebuff of Sir Hugh's hard, glacial silence, added gravely, "She loves you very much—in case you don't realize it" (238).

Thereafter, he is much kinder and more considerate in his behavior towards his daughter and, interestingly, the daughter who up until this time has been unable to "give her father up" begins to accept the attentions of her suitor.

Except in the important matter of the child, the heroine, as a rule, is extraordinarily timid in relation to her husband or lover. Often she is unable even to initiate a conversation with him:

> Once more I considered Joel's closed door. I supposed I should let him know I would no longer share an adjoining room. But I still didn't want to face him. A sense of indecision and foreboding held me back (*Spindrift*, 112).

The heroine's fearfulness is especially striking because she is often presented as brave, resourceful, and self-reliant until she falls in love. In a study of phobias in married women, Alexandra Symonds discusses several female patients who all seemed excessively self-reliant before marriage and after marriage became excessively helpless and unable to cope with the least stress or difficulty. She notes that these women all came from families who, for one reason or another, were "unable to respond to [the] child's needs." Hence the child learned to repress her childishness and developed "qualities that gave the illusion of strength."[49] Such women, however, are generally waiting for an opportuntity to give in to their feelings of helplessness and vulnerability. Marriage offers the prime opportunity because it provides a "socially acceptable" way for women to be utterly reliant on another. "Marriage then becomes their 'declaration of dependence.' If for any reason . . . the marriage does not seem to be all they expected they are in a panic and they cling even more."[50] The panic, the denial of their anger, the sense of being restricted all result in phobias. "They described their fears as fear of being closed in, a fear of being trapped, a fear that they would not be able to leave anytime they wanted to"[51]—in short, all the fears repeatedly expressed and often materially embodied in Gothics.

Symonds is struck by her patients' total "inability to communicate clearly to their partner." For, "since these are people who consider ordinary assertion to be the equivalent of hostility, they have an exaggerated fear" of any encounter which might "entail friction."[52] According to Symonds, the woman deals with her emotional turmoil—her repudiated aggression and her fear—by "externalizing," by making her husband into a "villain":[53] "[It] appears as though all her troubles would be over if only she had a different husband or if only someone else would get her husband to change."[54] This, more or less, is the typical Gothic "solution." The woman has either gotten involved with the wrong man, and the right man comes along and saves her from the villainy of the first man; or else the lover/husband "changes"—far from being the villain the heroine mistook him for, he is revealed to be the true hero. From then on, the heroine's troubles are over.

The constant splitting of male characteristics which occurs in the Gothics deserves comment. Russ, as I noted in the previous chapter, divides the men in the novels into two categories: the Super-Male and the Shadow-Male, the former almost always the apparent villain but the real hero, the latter usually a kind, considerate, gentle male who turns out to be vicious, insane, and/or murderous. The phenomenon of the "splitting of the male" in female literature has been little noted in feminist critical writings, yet it is a fascinating one and worthy of much attention. Feminists (as well as traditional psychoanalysts) have frequently cited the male tendency to divide women into two opposing and unreconcilable classes: the "spiritualized" mother and the whore.[55] But there is also a corresponding tendency in women to divide men into two classes: the omnipotent, domineering, aloof male and the gentle, but passive and fairly ineffectual male. (One of Meissner's female paranoid patients divided all men into "brutes" and "puppy dogs."[56]) This tendency has characterized the female Gothic since its inception. Not only is Montoni of *The Mysteries of Udolpho* the mirror image of the good father, but a further splitting also occurs along the lines we have been discussing. Whereas Montoni is a kind of forerunner of the "Super-Male," Valancourt is in many ways the prototype of the "Shadow-Male." Although Valancourt is, of course, not the villain of the piece, he is remarkably incapable of affording Emily any protection either against the domineering "mother," or, later, against the brutality of the "father." He pays, however, quite dearly for his weakness by being forced at the end of the novel to undergo a long trial during which he must prove himself worthy of Emily's love.

Interestingly, the female's tendency to classify men into two extreme categories is attributable to conflicts with the mother as well as with the father. Freedman observes that his female "paranoid" patients all looked for mates in possession "of an extremely unlikely combination of qualities":

He must, on the one hand, be passive and dependent enough in his orientation to the significant female in his life not to repeat the traumatic desertion [of the father]. On the other hand he must be strong enough to supply the kind of ego function that the patient felt she herself lacked and had had to derive from the maternal relation.[57]

Since the "combination of qualities" sought by these women was unrealizable, the patients all chose passive, reliable men who were not outstanding in any way (Shadow-Males, in effect).[58] This choice was in part determined by the father's early rejection of the patient and her consequent "inability to see herself as a person of sufficient potential and significance to hold the man she really admired."[59] But either alternative—the passive male or the strong, omnipotent male—is ultimately unsatisfactory, involving threats to the woman's weak sense of autonomy. The passive male—the Valancourt type—may be unable or unwilling to desert the woman, but his reluctance to assert himself may nevertheless result in feminine feelings of isolation. The strong male, like Montoni, may be capable of protecting the woman, but he is also capable of abusing and victimizing her. Valancourt is driven away from Emily by Madame Cheron (and doesn't return until Emily's adventures are almost at an end); Montoni kidnaps and tyrannizes over Emily and her aunt. In both cases separation anxieties remain unresolved, the woman is forced to retain her strong identification with the mother, and the male becomes an object of feminine resentment.

Modern Gothics usually solve this dilemma by endowing one man with the "unlikely combination of qualities" described by Freedman. In most cases, the feared omnipotent male is shown to have unsuspected reserves of tenderness and love:

The victory came in less than five seconds. She felt him relax, saw his eyes soften, felt his mouth curve in a smile, and she knew for the first time that there would be no more dread of the Distant Mood, no more tension and worry because she did not understand or could not cope with his changes of humor (*Shore*, 222–23).

Thus the admired male—the "father"—who had formerly been perceived as remote and rejecting, finally accepts the heroine, releasing her from the uncomfortable identification with the mother and simultaneously supplying the strength the heroine lacks. Moreover, by making either the feminized (Shadow) male or, occasionally, a woman, responsible for the crimes committed in the story, Gothics further reinforce women's distance from their "victimized" mothers, "proving" that men—"real men," at any rate—are not tyrants and brutes.

IV

Although I have been analyzing Gothics in the light of what is usually seen to be a psychic illness—paranoia—I have not done so in order to show up Gothic readers as neurotic and unstable. Many analysts have stressed that the paranoid process plays an inevitable part in human psychological development. "[P]aranoid traits may be quite mild, are almost universal and are often found in persons whose ego strengths may be otherwise quite sound."[60] And Freedman's study of paranoid women, like Wolowitz's study of the hysterical character referred to in the previous chapter, concludes by pointing out the similarity between his patients' attitudes and "the orientation . . . still generally considered appropriate . . . for women in some areas of Western Culture."[61] My analysis of Gothic Romances is meant to confirm and expand this claim. The structure of the Western family, with its unequal distribution of power, almost inevitably generates the kinds of feminine conflicts and anxieties we have been discussing.

Gothics, then, are expressions of the "normal" feminine paranoid personality, just as Harlequins are in some ways expressions of the "normal" feminine hysterical character. Further, each kind of text may be seen to relate to two basic anxieties, guilt and fear. The following distinction drawn by one analyst between the "depressive" and the "paranoid" type suggestively defines the positions of both the heroines and the readers of our two texts:

> The paranoid individual faces physical persecution (as in dreams of being attacked by murderous figures) while the depressed individual faces moral persecution (as, for example, in feeling surrounded by accusing eyes and pointing fingers), so that Klein regards both positions as setting up a primary anxiety.[62]

From the very beginnings of the novel, the two most popular forms for women have centered around these two "primary anxieties." We have seen how romances are centrally (though often only implicitly) concerned with the issue of guilt, how the plot of the very first romance, *Pamela*, focused on the moral persecution of the heroine, and how moral persecution continued even outside the book, as Fielding and others pointed accusing fingers at the "sham" heroine. *The Mysteries of Udolpho*, on the other hand, introduced the plot of the physically persecuted heroine surrounded by murderous figures.

"Blaming" is a characteristic of both the depressive and the paranoid position, but in the former the blame is directed at the self, whereas in the latter it is placed on someone outside the self:

> Paradoxically, in the depressive state, it is the aggressive introject which is retained and which forms the basis for the patient's self-blaming. Conversely, in the paranoid condition, it is the depressive introject which is retained, and the aggressive component which is projected externally and which is then seen as the agency of blame. . . . *Thus in the depressive state the patient is both victim and victimizer, but in the paranoid state he is able to regard himself more purely as only a victim* (emphasis added).[63]

This distinction has relevance for the two types of feminine narrative under discussion. The reader of Gothics, as compared to the reader of romance, is able to regard herself "more purely as only a victim." In considering the point of view of romances, we saw how the combination of personal and apersonal narration reinforced feminine guilt feelings by making the reader feel as if female "victims" are partial agents of their own "victimization" (i.e. seductions). Gothics are often written in the first person, allowing for a more direct identification with the heroine. And even though Gothics may occasionally employ third person narration, we don't encounter the same difficulties we did in Harlequins. Because Gothics have evolved such complex mechanisms as externalization, projection, doubling, and splitting, they permit women to experience hostile emotions without forcing them to see this hostility turned against themselves. Women in Gothics are persecuted, to be sure, but the persecution is not, as in romances, experienced as half-pleasurable. The Gothic heroine, unlike the romantic heroine, is not destined to turn her victimization into a triumph; she has not fallen in love with her victimizer (although she may for a time *think* she has; nevertheless she must have proof that this is *not* the case in order to "make her existence endurable"). In Gothics, then, feminine resentment is fully justified and, instead of being sabotaged by the woman herself, is satisfied through locating and punishing a "criminal" outside the self.

This distinction helps us to understand why Gothics have, since the eighteenth century, proved very attractive to many women writers, including avowed feminists. For Gothics probe the deepest layers of the feminine unconscious, providing a way for women to work through profound psychic conflicts, especially ambivalence towards the significant people in their lives—mothers, fathers, lovers. And furthermore, in the hands of a writer like Mary Wollstonecraft, the genre is used to explore these conflicts in relation to a society which systematically oppresses women. In other words, the Gothic has been used to drive home the "core of truth" in feminine paranoid fears and to connect the social with the psychological, the personal with the political. It has been used to show how women are at least potentially "pure victims," but how, in coming to view themselves as such, they perpetuate the cycle of victimization which occurs between fathers and mothers, mothers and daughters.

In Wollstonecraft's *Maria, Or the Wrongs of Woman*, for example, the insane asylum in which Maria is imprisoned is not simply a physical embodiment of her fears of entrapment; it is also a real insane asylum, into which her husband has had the legal right to place her in order to gain control of her fortune. One of Maria's greatest anxieties during her imprisonment concerns her daughter's fate. We have seen how Gothics in part serve to convince women that they will not be victims the way their mothers were and to provide a means by which women can work through their hostility towards their relativley unavailable (because "victimized") mothers and also, perhaps, develop some tolerance for their mothers' difficulties. The longest section in *Maria* is a letter written by her to her daughter in which she tries to explain the social and psychological factors leading up to her imprisonment and hence her seeming "abandonment" of her daughter. Thus Maria hopes to obtain her daughter's forgiveness and to break the chain of victimization handed down from one generation to the next.

In the letter Maria carefully shows how the circumstances we have discussed in this essay contributed to her present helplessness: social isolation ("Gain experience—ah! gain it—while experience is worth having");[64] and a father who tyrannized over the mother ("He was to be instantly obeyed, especially by my mother, whom he very benevolently married for love; but took care to remind her of the obligation, when she dared, in the slightest instance, to question his absolute authority.")[65] As in many of the Gothics we have been discussing, Maria marries a man who seems gentle, kind, and supportive, but who turns out to be brutal and tyrannical. Finally he has Maria committed to an insane asylum so that he can legally obtain her money. In this prison, Maria meets Henry Darnford, a man who on one occasion had saved her from the tyrannies of her husband and whom she desperately tries to invest with the "unlikely combination of qualities" of a Super-Male: "Pygmalion formed an ivory maid, and longed for an informing soul. She, on the contrary, combined all the qualities of a hero's mind, and fate presented a statue in which she might enshrine them."[66] But, unlike the endings of popular Gothics, the fantasy ending is not destined to work out. Wollstonecraft died before she could finish her novel, but it is clear from the notes she left that she intended Darnford to betray and abandon Maria.

The difference between popular Gothics—usually dismissed as escapist and trivial literature—and a militantly feminist Gothic novel like *Maria* is that the latter explores on a conscious level conflicts which popular Gothics exploit, yet keep at an unconscious level. Popular Gothics resolve the conflicts through a fantasy ending, whereas the ending of *Maria* leaves the conflicts unresolved. Yet both types of Gothic testify to women's extreme discontent with the social and psychological processes which transform them into victims. For it ought to be clear by now that although modern Gothics may frequently contain statements endorsing notions of feminine self-sacrifice, the workings of the plot actually run counter to such professions. In other words, modern Gothics may inform us that "mutilation" is "truly the gift of gifts," but they also assure us, to our immense relief, that it won't be extracted from us.

IV

The Search for Tomorrow
in Today's Soap Operas

I

Approximately twelve soap operas are shown daily, each half an hour to an hour and a half long. The first of them goes on the air at about 10:00 a.m., and they run almost continuously until about 3:30 p.m. (of course, the times vary according to local programming schedules). In 1975 the *New York Times Magazine* reported that 20 million people watch soap operas daily, the average program attracting 6.7 million viewers, almost 90 percent of them female. Further:

> The households break down economically and educationally in proportions similar to the population as a whole—51.3 percent with household incomes under $10,000, for instance, and 23.9 percent with incomes over $15,000. About 24.8 percent of household heads have only an elementary school education, while 56.2 percent have a high school education or better. . . . The programs gross more than $300-million a year from the makers of soaps, deodorants, cake mixes and other household products, providing a disproportionate share of network profits though nighttime budgets are much larger.[1]

With the exception of "Ryan's Hope," which takes place in a big city, the soap operas are set in small towns and involve two or three families intimately connected with one another. Families are often composed of several generations, and the proliferation of generations is accelerated by the propensity of soap opera characters to mature at an incredibly rapid rate; thus, the matriarch on *Days of Our Lives*, who looks to be about 65, has managed over

85

the years to become a great-great-grandmother. Sometimes on a soap opera one of the families will be fairly well to do, and another somewhat lower on the social scale though still, as a rule, identifiably middle-class. In any case, since there is so much intermingling and intermarrying, class distinctions quickly become hopelessly blurred. Children figure largely in many of the plots, but they don't appear on the screen all that often; nor do the very old. Blacks and other minorities are almost completely excluded.

Women as well as men frequently work outside the home, usually in professions such as law and medicine, and women are generally on a professional par with men. But most of everyone's time is spent experiencing and discussing personal and domestic crises. Kathryn Weibel lists "some of the most frequent themes":

> the evil woman
> the great sacrifice
> the winning back of an estranged lover/spouse
> marrying her for her money, respectability, etc.
> the unwed mother
> deceptions about the paternity of children
> career vs. housewife
> the alcoholic woman (and occasionally man).[2]

Controversial social problems are introduced from time to time: rape was recently an issue on several soap operas and was, for the most part, handled in a sensitive manner. In spite of the fact that soap operas contain more references to social problems than do most other forms of mass entertainment, critics tend to fault them heavily for their lack of social realism.

If television is considered by some to be a vast wasteland, soap operas are thought to be the least nourishing spot in the desert. The surest way to damn a film, a television program, or even a situation in real life is to invoke an analogy to soap operas. In the same way that men are often concerned to show that what they are, above all, is not women, not "feminine," so television programs and movies will, surprisingly often, tell us that they are not soap operas. On a recent "Phil Donahue Show," a group of handicapped Vietnam War Veterans were bitterly relating their experiences; at one point Donahue interrupted the conversation to assure his audience (comprised almost entirely of women) that he was not giving them soap opera, but he thought it important to "personalize" the war experience. An afternoon "Money Movie," *Middle of the Night,* an interminable Paddy Chayevsky affair starring Frederick March, dealt with one man's life-crisis as, on the brink of old age, he falls in love with a very young Kim Novak and struggles against the petty and destructive jealousy of his sister and daughter. "This is *not* a soap opera," he reprimands the sister at one point. Since to me it had all the ingredients of one, I could only conclude that men's soap operas are not to be thought of as soap operas only because they are *for men* (or about men).

It is refreshing, therefore, to read Horace Newcomb's book, *T.V.: The Most Popular Art,* in which he suggests that far from being the nadir of art forms, as most people take them to be, soap operas represent in some ways the furthest advance of T.V. art. In other words, for all their stereotypical qualities, they combine to the highest degree two of the most important elements of the television aesthetic: "intimacy" and "continuity." Television, says Newcomb, is uniquely suited to deal with character and interpersonal relations rather than with action and setting. Soap operas, of course, play exclusively on the intimate properties of the medium. Newcomb also points out that because of the serial nature of the programs television can offer us depictions of people in situations which grow and change over time, allowing for a greater "audience involvement, a sense of becoming a part of the lives and actions of the characters they see."[3] Thus far it is mainly soap opera which has taken advantage of these possibilities for continuity, nighttime programs, by and large, tending to "forget" from week to week all of the conflicts and lessons which have gone before.

Newcomb's book is important in that, by refusing to indulge in an anti-feminine bias against soap operas, it reveals a new way of seeing these programs which allows them to be placed in the vanguard of T.V. aesthetics (dubious as this distinction may seem to many people). My approach is different from, though in no sense opposed to Newcomb's. I propose not to ignore what is "feminine" about soap operas but to focus on it, to show how they provide a unique narrative pleasure which, while it has become thoroughly adapted to the rhythms of women's lives in the home, provides an alternative to the dominant "pleasures of the text" analyzed by Roland Barthes and others. Soap operas may be in the vanguard not just of T.V. art but of all popular narrative art.

II

Whereas the meaning of Harlequin Romances depends almost entirely on the sense of an ending, soap operas are important to their viewers in part because they never end. Whereas Harlequins encourage our identification with one character, soap operas invite identification with numerous personalities. And whereas Harlequins are structured around two basic enigmas, in soap operas, the enigmas proliferate: "Will Bill find out that his wife's sister's baby is really his by artificial insemination? Will his wife submit to her sister's blackmail attempts, or will she finally let Bill know the truth? If he discovers the truth, will this lead to another nervous breakdown, causing him to go back to Springfield General where his ex-wife and his illegitimate daughter are both doctors and sworn enemies?" Tune in tomorrow, not in order to find out the answers, but to see what further complications will defer the resolutions and introduce new questions. Thus the narrative, by placing ever more complex obstacles between desire and fulfillment, makes anticipation of an end an end in itself. Soap operas invest exquisite pleasure in the central condition of a woman's life: waiting—whether for her phone to ring, for the baby to take its nap, or for the family to be reunited shortly after the day's final soap opera has left *its* family still struggling against dissolution.

According to Roland Barthes, the hermeneutic code, which propounds the enigmas, functions by making "expectation . . . the basic condition for truth: truth, these narratives tell us, is what is *at the end* of expectation. This design implies a return to order, for expectation is a disorder."[4] But, of course, soap operas do not end. Consequently, truth for women is seen to lie not "at the end of expectation," but *in* expectation, not in the "return to order," but in (familial) disorder.

Many critics have considered endings to be crucial to narratives. Frank Kermode speculates that fictive ends are probably "figures" for death.[5] In his essay on 'The Storyteller," Walter Benjamin comes to a similar conclusion:

> The novel is significant . . . not because it presents someone else's fate to us, perhaps didactically, but because this stranger's fate by virtue of the flame which consumes it yields us the warmth which we never draw from our own fate. What draws the reader to the novel

is the hope of warming his shivering life with a death he reads about.[6]

But soap operas offer the promise of immortality and eternal return—same time tomorrow. Although at first glance, soap opera seems in this respect to be diametrically opposed to the female domestic novels of the nineteenth century, which were preoccupied with death, especially the deaths of infants and small children, a second look tells us that the fantasy of immortality embodied in modern melodrama is not so very different from the fantasies expressed in the older works. In the latter, it is not the case that, in Benjamin's words, "the 'meaning' of a character's life is revealed only in his death";[7] rather, for women writers and readers, forced to endure repeatedly the premature loss of their children, it was the meaning of the character's death that had to be ascertained, and this meaning was revealed only in the afterlife, only in projections of eternity.

"[T]racts of time unpunctuated by meaning derived from the end are not to be borne," says Frank Kermode, confidently.[8] But perhaps for women (no doubt for men too) certain kinds of endings are attended by a sense of meaninglessness even less capable of being borne than limitless expanses of time which at least hold open the possibility that something may sometime happen to confer sense upon the present. The loss of a child was, for nineteenth century women, an example of such an unbearable ending: it was, as Helen Papashvily has called it, "a double tragedy—the loss of a precious individual and the negation of her creativity,"[9] and it threatened, perhaps more than any other experience, to give the lie to the belief in a benevolent God and the ultimate rightness of the world order. And so, it was necessary to believe that the child would join a heavenly family for all eternity.

For twentieth-century woman, the loss of her family, not through death, but through abandonment (children growing up and leaving home) is perhaps another "ending" which is feared because it leaves women lonely and isolated and without significant purpose in life. The fear, as Barbara Easton persuasively argues, is not without foundation:

> With the geographical mobility and breakdown of communities of the twentieth century, women's support networks outside the family have weakened, and they are likely to turn to their husbands for intimacy that earlier

89

generations would have found elsewhere.[10]

The family is, for many women, their only support, and soap operas offer the assurance of its immortality.[11] They present the viewer with a picture of a family which, though it is always in the process of breaking down, stays together no matter how intolerable its situation may get. Or, perhaps more accurately, the family remains close precisely because it is perpetually in a chaotic state. The unhappiness generated by the family can only be solved in the family. Misery becomes not, as in many nineteenth-century women's novels, the consequence and sign of the family's breakdown, but the very means of its functioning and perpetuation. As long as the children are unhappy, as long as things *don't* come to a satisfying conclusion, the mother will be needed as confidante and adviser, and her function will never end.

One critic of soap opera remarks, "If . . . as Aristotle so reasonably claimed, drama is the imitation of a human action that has a beginning, a middle, and an end, soap opera belongs to a separate genus that is entirely composed of an indefinitely expandable middle."[12] It is not only that successful soap operas do not end, it is also that they cannot end. In *The Complete Soap Opera Book*, an interesting and lively work on the subject, the authors show how a radio serial forced off the air by television tried to wrap up its story.[13] It was an impossible task. Most of the storyline had to be discarded and only one element could be followed through to its end—an important example of a situation in which what Barthes calls the "discourse's instinct for preservation" has virtually triumphed over authorial control.[14] Furthermore, it is not simply that the story's completion would have taken too long for the amount of time allotted by the producers. More importantly, I believe it would have been impossible to resolve the contradiction between the imperatives of melodrama—the good must be rewarded and the wicked punished—and the latent message of soap operas— everyone cannot be happy at the same time, no matter how deserving they are. The claims of any two people, especially in love matters, are often mutually exclusive.

John Cawelti defines melodrama as having

> at its center the moral fantasy of showing forth the essential 'rightness' of the world order. . . . Because of this, melodramas are usually rather complicated in plot

and character; instead of identifying with a single protagonist through his line of action, the melodrama
typically makes us intersect imaginatively with many
lives. Subplots multiply, and the point of view continually shifts in order to involve us in a complex of
destinies. Through this complex of characters and plots
we see not so much the working of individual fates but
the underlying moral process of the world.[15]

It is scarcely an accident that this essentially nineteenth-century
form continues to appeal strongly to women, whereas the classic
(male) narrative film is, as Laura Mulvey points out, structured
"around a main controlling figure with whom the spectator can
identify."[16] Soap operas continually insist on the insignificance of
the individual life. A viewer might at one moment be asked to identify with a woman finally reunited with her lover, only to have that
identification broken in a moment of intensity and attention
focused on the sufferings of the woman's rival.

If, as Mulvey claims, the identification of the spectator with "a
main male protagonist" results in the spectator's becoming "the rep-
resentative of power,"[17] the multiple identification which occurs in
soap opera results in the spectator's being divested of power. For
the spectator is never permitted to identify with a character com-
pleting an entire action. Instead of giving us one "powerful ideal
ego . . . who can make things happen and control events better
than the subject/spectator can,"[18] soap operas present us with numerous limited egos, each in conflict with the others, and continually
thwarted in its attempts to control events because of inadequate
knowledge of other peoples' plans, motivations, and schemes.
Sometimes, indeed, the spectator, frustrated by the sense of powerlessness induced by soap operas, will, like an interfering mother,
try to control events directly:

> Thousands and thousands of letters [from soap fans to
> actors] give advice, warn the heroine of impending
> doom, caution the innocent to beware of the nasties
> ("Can't you see that your brother-in-law is up to no
> good?"), inform one character of another's doings, or
> reprimand a character for unseemly behavior.[19]

Presumably, this intervention is ineffectual, and feminine powerlessness is reinforced on yet another level.

The subject/spectator of soap operas, it could be said, is constituted as a sort of ideal mother: a person who possesses greater wisdom than all her children, whose sympathy is large enough to encompass the conflicting claims of her family (she identifies with them all), and who has no demands or claims of her own (she identifies with no one character exclusively). The connection between melodrama and mothers is an old one. Harriet Beecher Stowe, of course, made it explicit in *Uncle Tom's Cabin*, believing that if her book could bring its female readers to see the world as one extended family, the world would be vastly improved. But in Stowe's novel, the frequent shifting of perspective identifies the reader with a variety of characters in order ultimately to ally her with the mother/author and with God who, in their higher wisdom and understanding, can make all the hurts of the world go away, thus insuring the "essential 'rightness' of the world order." Soap opera, however, denies the "mother" this extremely flattering illusion of her power. On the one hand, it plays upon the spectator's expectations of the melodramatic form, continually stimulating (by means of the hermeneutic code) the desire for a just conclusion to the story, and, on the other hand, it constantly presents the desire as unrealizable, by showing that conclusions only lead to further tension and suffering. Thus soap operas convince women that their highest goal is to see their families united and happy, while consoling them for their inability to realize this ideal and bring about familial harmony.

This is reinforced by the character of the good mother on soap operas. In contrast to the manipulating mother who tries to interfere with her children's lives, the good mother must sit helplessly by as her children's lives disintegrate; her advice, which she gives only when asked, is temporarily soothing, but usually ineffectual. Her primary function is to be sympathetic, to tolerate the foibles and errors of others. Maeve Ryan, the mother on "Ryan's Hope," is a perfect example. "Ryan's Hope," a soap opera centered around an Irish-Catholic, bar-owning family which, unlike the majority of soap families, lives in a large city, was originally intended to be more "realistic," more socially oriented than the majority of soap operas.[20] Nevertheless, the function of the mother is unchanged: she is there to console her children and try to understand them as they have illegitimate babies, separate from their spouses (miraculously obtaining annulments instead of divorces), and dispense birth control information in the poor neighborhoods.

It is important to recognize that soap operas serve to affirm the primacy of the family not by presenting an ideal family, but by portraying a family in constant turmoil and appealing to the spectator to be understanding and tolerant of the many evils which go on within that family. The spectator/mother, identifying with each character in turn, is made to see "the larger picture" and extend her sympathy to both the sinner and the victim. She is thus in a position to forgive all. As a rule, only those issues which can be tolerated and ultimately pardoned are introduced on soap operas. The list includes careers for women, abortions, premarital and extramarital sex, alcoholism, divorce, mental and even physical cruelty. An issue like homosexuality, which could explode the family structure rather than temporarily disrupt it, is simply ignored. Soap operas, contrary to many people's conception of them, are not conservative but liberal, and the mother is the liberal par excellence. By constantly presenting her with the many-sidedness of any question, by never reaching a permanent conclusion, soap operas undermine her capacity to form unambiguous judgments.

In this respect, soap opera melodrama can be said to create in the spectator a divisiveness of feeling totally different from the "monopathic" feeling Robert Heilman sees as constituting the appeal of traditional melodrama. There, he writes, "one enjoys the wholeness of a practical competence that leads to swift and sure action; one is untroubled by psychic fumbling, by indecisiveness, by awareness of alternate courses, by weak muscles or strong counterimperatives."[21] But in soap operas, we are constantly troubled by "psychic fumbling" and by "strong counterimperatives." To take one example, Trish, on "Days of Our Lives," takes her small son and runs away from her husband David in order to advance her singing career. When she gets an opportunity to go to London to star in a show, she leaves the child with her mother. When the show folds, she becomes desperate to get back home to see her child, but since she has no money, she has to prostitute herself. Finally she is able to return, and after experiencing a series of difficulties, she locates her son, who is now staying with his father. Once she is in town, a number of people, angry at the suffering she has caused David, are hostile and cruel towards her. Thus far, the story seems to bear out the contention of the critics who claim that soap opera characters who leave the protection of the family are unequivocally punished. But the matter is not so simple. For the unforgiving people are shown to have limited perspectives. The larger view is summed up by Margo, a woman who has a mysterious and perhaps fatal disease and who, moreover, has every reason to be jealous of Trish since Trish was the first love of Margo's husband. Margo claims that no one can ever fully know what private motives drove Trish to abandon her family; besides, she says, life is too short to bear grudges and inflict pain. The spectator, who sees the extremity of Trish's sorrow, assents. And at the same time, the spectator is made to forgive and understand the unforgiving characters, for she is intimately drawn into their anguish and suffering as well.

These remarks must be qualified. If soap operas keep us caring about everyone; if they refuse to allow us to condemn most characters and actions until all the evidence is in (and, of course, it never is), there is one character whom we are allowed to hate unreservedly: the villainess, the negative image of the spectator's ideal self.[22] Although much of the suffering on soap opera is presented as unavoidable, the surplus suffering is often the fault of the villainess who tries to "make things happen and control events better than the subject/spectator can." The villainess might very possibly be a mother trying to manipulate her children's lives or ruin their marriages. Or perhaps she is a woman avenging herself on her husband's family because it has never fully accepted her.

This character cannot be dismissed as easily as many critics seem to think.[23] The extreme delight viewers apparently take in despising the villainess testifies to the enormous amount of energy involved in the spectator's repression and to her (albeit unconscious) resentment at being constituted as an egoless receptacle for the suffering of others.[24] The villainess embodies the "split-off fury" which, in the words of Dorothy Dinnerstein, is "the underside of the 'truly feminine' woman's monstrously overdeveloped talent for unreciprocated empathy."[25] This aspect of melodrama can be traced back to the middle of the nineteenth century when *Lady Audley's Secret*, a drama based on Mary Elizabeth Braddon's novel about a governess turned bigamist and murderess, became one of the most popular stage melodramas of all time.[26] In her discussion of the novel, Elaine Showalter shows how the author, while paying lipservice to conventional notions about the feminine role, managed to appeal to "thwarted female energy":

> The brilliance of *Lady Audley's Secret* is that Braddon
> makes her would-be murderess the fragile blond angel

of domestic realism. . . . The dangerous woman is not
the rebel or the bluestocking, but the "pretty little girl"
whose indoctrination in the female role has taught her
secrecy and deceitfulness, almost as secondary sex
characteristics.[27]

Thus the villainess is able to transform traditional feminine
weaknesses into the sources of her strength.

Similarly, on soap operas, the villainess seizes those aspects of
a woman's life which normally render her most helpless and tries to
turn them into weapons for manipulating other characters. She is,
for instance, especially good at manipulating pregnancy, unlike
most women, who, as Mary Ellmann wittily points out, tend to feel
manipulated by it:

> At the same time, women cannot help observing that
> conception (their highest virtue, by all reports) simply
> happens or doesn't. It lacks the style of enterprise. It can
> be prevented by foresight and device (though success
> here, as abortion rates show, is exaggerated), but it is
> accomplished by luck (good or bad). Purpose often
> seems, if anything, a deterrent. A devious business ben-
> efitting by indirection, by pretending not to care, as
> though the self must trick the body. In the regrettable
> conception, the body instead tricks the self—much as it
> does in illness or death.[28]

In contrast to the numerous women on soap operas who are either
trying unsuccessfully to become pregnant or who have become
pregnant as a consequence of a single unguarded moment in their
lives, the villainess manages, for a time at least, to make pregnancy
work for her. She gives it the "style of enterprise." If she decides she
wants to marry a man, she will take advantage of him one night
when he is feeling especially vulnerable and seduce him. And if she
doesn't achieve the hoped-for pregnancy, undaunted, she simply
lies to her lover about being pregnant. The villainess thus reverses
male/female roles: anxiety about conception is transferred to the
male. He is the one who had better watch his step and curb his pro-
miscuous desires or he will find himself burdened with an unwanted child.

Some episodes on 'The Young and the Restless" perfectly illustrate the point. Lori's sister Leslie engages in a one night sexual encounter with Lori's husband, Lance. Of course, she becomes pregnant as a result. Meanwhile Lori and Lance have been having marital difficulties, and Lori tries to conceive a child, hoping this will bring her closer to her husband. When she finds out about her sister and Lance, she becomes frantic about her inability to conceive, realizing that if Lance ever finds out he is the father of Leslie's child, he well be drawn to Leslie and reject her. Vanessa, Lance's mother and a classic villainess, uses her knowledge of the situation to play on Lori's insecurities and drive a wedge between her and Lance. At the same time, Lori's father has been seduced by Jill Foster, another villainess, who immediately becomes pregnant, thus forcing him to marry her.

Furthermore, the villainess, far from allowing her children to rule her life, often uses them in order to further her own selfish ambitions. One of her typical ploys is to threaten the father or the woman possessing custody of the child with the deprivation of that child. She is the opposite of the woman at home, who at first is forced to have her children constantly with her, and later is forced to let them go—for a time on a daily recurring basis and then permanently. The villainess enacts for the spectator a kind of reverse *fort-da* game, in which the mother is the one who attempts to send the child away and bring it back at will, striving to overcome feminine passivity in the process of the child's appearance and loss.[29] Into the bargain, she also tries to manipulate the man's disappearance and return by keeping the fate of his child always hanging in the balance. And again, male and female roles tend to get reversed: the male suffers the typically feminine anxiety over the threatened absence of his children. On "Ryan's Hope," for example, Delia continually uses her son to control her husband and his family. At one point she clashes with another villainess, Raye Woodward, over the child and the child's father, Frank Ryan, from whom Delia is divorced. Raye realizes that the best way to get Frank interested in her is by taking a maternal interest in his child. When Delia uncovers Raye's scheme, she becomes determined to foil it by regaining custody of the boy. On "The Young and the Restless," to take another example, Derek is on his way out of the house to try to intercept Jill Foster on her way to the altar and persuade her to marry him instead of Stuart Brooks. Derek's ex-wife Suzanne thwarts the attempt by choosing that moment to inform him that their son is in a mental hospital.

The villainess thus continually works to make the most out of events which render other characters totally helpless. Literal paralysis turns out, for one villainess, to be an active blessing, since it prevents her husband from carrying out his plans to leave her; when she gets back the use of her legs, therefore, she doesn't tell anyone. And even death doesn't stop another villainess from wreaking havoc; she returns to haunt her husband and convince him to try to kill his new wife.

The popularity of the villainess would seem to be explained in part by the theory of repetition compulsion, which Freud saw as resulting from the individual's attempt to become an active manipulator of her/his own powerlessness.[30] The spectator, it might be thought, continually tunes into soap operas to watch the villainess as she tries to gain control over her feminine passivity, thereby acting out the spectator's fantasies of power. Of course, most formula stories (like the Western) appeal to the spectator/reader's compulsion to repeat: the spectator constantly returns to the same story in order to identify with the main character and achieve, temporarily, the illusion of mastery denied him or her in real life. But soap operas refuse the spectator even this temporary illusion of mastery. The villainess's painstaking attempts to turn her powerlessness to her own advantage are always thwarted just when victory seems most assured, and she must begin her machinations all over again. Moreover, the spectator does not comfortably identify with the villainess. Since the spectator despises the villainess as the negative image of her ideal self, she not only watches the villainess act out her own hidden wishes, but simultaneously sides with the forces conspiring against fulfillment of those wishes. As a result of this "internal contestation,"[31] the spectator comes to enjoy repetition for its own sake and takes her adequate pleasure in the building up and tearing down of the plot. In this way, perhaps, soap operas help reconcile her to the meaningless, repetitive nature of much of her life and work within the home.

Soap operas, then, while constituting the spectator as a "good mother," provide in the person of the villainess an outlet for feminine anger: in particular, as we have seen, the spectator has the satisfaction of seeing men suffer the same anxieties and guilt that women usually experience and seeing them receive similar kinds of punishment for their transgressions. But that anger is neutralized at every moment in that it is the special object of the spectator's hatred. The spectator, encouraged to sympathize with almost everyone, can vent her frustration on the one character who refuses to accept her own powerlessness, who is unashamedly self-seeking. Woman's anger is directed at woman's anger, and an eternal cycle is created.

And yet, if the villainess never succeeds, if, in accordance with the spectator's conflicting desires, she is doomed to eternal repetition, then she obviously never permanently fails either. When, as occasionally happens, a villainess reforms, a new one immediately supplants her. Generally, however, a popular villainess will remain true to her character for most or all of the soap opera's duration. And if the villainess constantly suffers because she is always foiled, we should remember that she suffers no more than the good characters, who don't even try to interfere with their fates. Again, this may be contrasted to the usual imperatives of melodrama, which demand an ending to justify the suffering of the good and punish the wicked. While soap operas thrive they present a continual reminder that women's anger is alive, if not exactly well.

III

Critics have speculated before now about why the narrative form of soap opera seems to have special appeal to women. Marcia Kinder, reviewing Ingmar Bergman's *Scenes from a Marriage*, suggests that the "open-ended, slow paced, multi-climaxed" structure of soap opera is "in tune with patterns of female sexuality."[32] While this is certainly a plausible explanation, it should be clear by now that soap opera as a narrative form also reflects and cultivates the "proper" psychological disposition of the woman in the home. Nancy Chodorow provides us with a nice description of women's work in the home and usefully contrasts it to work performed in the labor force:

> Women's activities in the home involve continuous connection to and concern about children and attunement to adult masculine needs, both of which require connection to, rather than separateness from, others. The work of maintenance and reproduction is characterized by its repetitive and routine continuity, and does not involve specified sequence or progression. By contrast, work in

the labor force—"men's work"—is likely to be contrac-
tual, to be more specifically delimited, and to contain a
notion of defined progression and product.[33]

We have already seen ways in which soap operas encourage
women to become involved in—"connected to"—the lives of the
people on the screen. A comparison with *Dallas*, the popular nighttime serial, is instructive. There, the characters are highly glamor-
ized, the difference between their world and that of the average
viewer could not be greater, and the difference is continually emphasized. On soap operas, by contrast, glamour and wealth are
played down. Characters are attractive enough so that their looks
are not distracting, well off enough so that, as in a Henry James
novel, they can worry about more exciting problems than inflation
at the market. But glamour and wealth are not preoccupations as
they are on *Dallas*. Obviously, the soap opera world is in reality no
more like the average spectator's than the world of *Dallas*; yet the
characters and the settings all connote, to use a Barthesian type of
neologism, averageness. This accounts for the fans' frequent contention that soap opera characters are just like them—whereas
no one is likely to make such a claim about the Ewing family on
Dallas. The consequent blurring of the boundaries between fantasy
and life which sometimes occurs (as, for example, when fans write
letters to the "characters," giving them advice about their problems) suggests that the psychological fusion which Chodorow says
is experienced by the wife/mother applies in these instances to the
viewer's experience of the characters.

Another way in which soap opera stimulates women's desire
for connectedness is through the constant, claustrophobic use of
close-up shots. Often only the audience is privileged to witness the
characters' expressions, which are complex and intricately coded,
signifying triumph, bitterness, despair, confusion—the entire emotional register, in fact. Soap operas contrast sharply with other
popular forms aimed at masculine visual pleasure, which is often
centered on the fragmentation and fetishization of the female body.
In the most popular feminine visual art, it is easy to forget that
characters even have bodies, so insistently are close-ups of faces
employed. One critic significantly remarks, "A face in close-up is
what before the age of film only a lover or a mother ever saw."[34]
Soap operas appear to be the one visual art which activates the gaze
of the mother—but in order to provoke anxiety about the welfare

of others. Close-ups provide the spectator with training in "reading" other people, in being sensitive to their (unspoken) feelings at any given moment.

Chodorow stresses the "connectedness" of women's work in the home, but this is only half the picture. The wife's job is further complicated by the fact that she must often deal with several people with different, perhaps conflicting moods; and further she must be prepared to drop what she is doing in order to cope with various conflicts and problems the moment they arise. Unlike most workers in the labor force, the housewife must beware of concentrating her energies exclusively on any one task—otherwise, the dinner could burn or the baby could crack its skull (as happened once on "Ryan's Hope" when the villainess became so absorbed in a love encounter that she forgot to keep an eye on her child). The housewife functions, as many creative women have sadly realized, by distraction. Tillie Olsen writes in *Silences*, "More than in any other human relationship, overwhelmingly more, motherhood means being instantly interruptable, responsive, responsible. . . . It is distraction, not meditation, that becomes habitual: interruption, not continuity; spasmodic, not constant toil."[35] Daytime television plays a part in habituating women to distraction, interruption, and spasmodic toil.

These observations have crucial implications for current television theory. In his book *Television: Technology and Cultural Form* Raymond Williams suggests that the shifts in television programming from one type of show to another and from part of a show to a commercial should not be seen as "interruptions"—of a mood, of a story—but as parts of a whole. What at first appear to be discrete programming units in fact interrelate in profound and complex ways. Williams uses the term "flow" to describe this interaction of various programs with each other and with commercials. "The fact of flow," he says, defines the "central television experience."[36] Against Williams I would argue that the flow within soap operas as well as between soap operas and other programming units reinforces the very principle of interruptability crucial to the proper functioning of women in the home. In other words, what Williams calls "the central television experience" is a profoundly decentering experience.

"The art of being off center," wrote Walter Benjamin in an essay on Baudelaire, "in which the little man could acquire training in places like the Fun Fair, flourished concomitantly with unemployment."[37] Soap operas also provide training in the "art of being off center" (and we should note in passing that it is probably no accident that the nighttime "soap opera" *Dallas* and its spinoffs and imitators are flourishing in a period of economic crisis and rising unemployment). The housewife, of course, is in one sense, like the little man at the Fun Fair, unemployed, but in another sense she is perpetually employed—her work, like a soap opera, is never done. Moreover, as I have said, her duties are split among a variety of domestic and familial tasks, and her television programs keep her from desiring a focused existence by involving her in the pleasures of a fragmented life.

Interruptions may be, as Benjamin thought, one of the fundamental devices of all art, but surely soap opera relies on them to a far greater extent than any other art.[38] Revelations, confrontations, and reunions are constantly being interrupted and postponed by telephone calls, unexpected visitors, counterrevelations, catastrophes, and switches from one plot to another. These interruptions are both annoying and pleasurable: if we are torn away from one exciting story, we at least have the relief of picking up the thread of an unfinished one. Like the (ideal) mother in the home, we are kept interested in a number of events at once and are denied the luxury of a total and prolonged absorption. Commercials constitute another kind of interruption, in this case from *outside* the diegesis. Commercials present the housewife with mini-problems and their resolutions, so after witnessing all the agonizingly hopeless dilemmas on soap operas, the spectator has the satisfaction of seeing something cleaned up, if only a stained shirt or a dirty floor.

Although daytime commercials and soap operas are both set overwhelmingly within the home, the two views of the home seem antithetical, for the chief concerns of commercials are precisely the ones soap operas censor out. The saggy diapers, yellow wax build-up and carpet smells making up the world of daytime television ads are rejected by soap operas in favor of "Another World," as the very title of one soap opera announces, a world in which characters deal only with the "large" problems of human existence: crime, love, death and dying. But this antithesis embodies a deep truth about the way women function in (or, more accurately, around) culture: as both moral and spiritual guides and household drudges: now one, now the other, moving back and forth between the extremes, but obviously finding them difficult to reconcile.[39]

Similarly, the violent mood swings the spectator undergoes in switching from quiz shows, the other popular daytime television fare, to soap operas also constitute a kind of interruption, just as the housewife is required to endure monotonous, repetitive work but to be able to switch instantly and on demand from her role as a kind of bedmaking, dishwashing automaton to a large sympathizing consciousness. It must be stressed that while nighttime television certainly affords shifts in mood, notably from comedy to drama, these shifts are not nearly as extreme as in daytime programming. Quiz shows present the spectator with the same game, played and replayed frenetically day after day, with each game a self-contained unit, crowned by climactic success or failure. Soap operas, by contrast, endlessly defer resolutions and climaxes and undercut the very notion of success.

The formal properties of daytime televison thus accord closely with the rhythms of women's work in the home. Individual soap operas as well as the flow of various programs and commercials tend to make repetition, interruption, and distraction pleasurable. But we can go even further and note that for women viewers reception itself often takes place in a state of distraction. According to Benjamin, "reception in a state of distraction . . . finds in the film its true means of exercise."[40] But now that we have television we can see that it goes beyond film in this respect, or at least the daytime programs do. For, the consumption of most films as well as of nighttime programs in some ways recapitulates the work situation in the factory or office: the viewer is physically passive, immobilized, and all his attention is focused on the object before him. Even the most allegedly "mindless" program requires a fairly strong degree of concentration if its plot is to make sense. But since the housewife's "leisure" time is not so strongly demarcated, her entertainment must often be consumed on the job. As the authors of *The Complete Soap Opera Book* tell us:

> The typical fan was assumed to be trotting about her daily chores with her mop in one hand, duster in the other, cooking, tending babies, answering telephones. Thus occupied, she might not be able to bring her full powers of concentration to bear on *Backstage Wife*.[41]

This accounts, in part, for the "realistic" feel of soap operas. The script writers, anticipating the housewife's distracted state, are careful to repeat important elements of the story several times.

Thus, if two characters are involved in a confrontation which is supposed to mark a final break in their relationship, that same confrontation must be repeated, with minor variations, a few times in order to make sure the viewer gets the point. "Clean breaks"—surely a supreme fiction—are impossible on soap operas.

Benjamin, writing of film, invoked architecture as the traditional art most closely resembling the new one in the kinds of response they elicit. Both are mastered to some extent in a state of distraction: that is, both are appropriated "not so much by attention as by habit."[42] It is interesting to recall in this connection the Dadaist Eric Satie's concept of furniture music, which would be absorbed while people went about their business or chatted with each other. Television is the literalization of the metaphor of furniture art, but it must be stressed that this art is more than simply background noise in the way, for example, that muzak is; soap operas are intensely meaningful to many women, as a conversation with any fan will immediately confirm.

Ironically, critics of television untiringly accuse its viewers of indulging in escapism. In other words, both high art critics and politically oriented critics, though motivated by different concerns, unite in condemning daytime television for *distracting* the housewife from her real situation. My point has been that a distracted or distractable frame of mind is crucial to the housewife's efficient functioning *in* her real situation, and at this level television and its so-called distractions, along with the particular forms they take, are intimately bound up with women's work.

IV

Given the differences in the ways men and women experience their lives, it is not surprising to find that "narrative pleasure" can sometimes mean very different things to men and women. This is an important point. Too often feminist criticism implies that there is only one kind of pleasure to be derived from narrative and that it is an essentially masculine one. Hence, it is further implied, feminist artists must first of all challenge this pleasure and then out of nothing begin to construct a feminist aesthetics and feminist form. This is a mistaken position, in my view, for it keeps us constantly in an adversary role, always on the defensive, always, as it were, complaining about the family but never leaving home. Feminist artists don't have to start from nothing; rather, they can look for clues to women's pleasure which are already present in existing forms, even if this pleasure is currently placed at the service of patriarchy. Claire Johnston, a feminist film theorist, has argued for a strategy combining "both the notion of film as a political tool and film as entertainment":

> For too long these have been regarded as two opposing poles with little common ground. In order to counter our objectification in the cinema, our collective fantasies must be released: women's cinema must embody the working through of desire: such an objective demands the use of the entertainment film. Ideas derived from the entertainment film, then, should inform the political film, and political ideas should inform the entertainment cinema: a two way process.[43]

Clearly, women find soap operas eminently entertaining, and an analysis of the pleasure these programs afford can provide feminists with ways not only to challenge this pleasure but to incorporate it into their own artistic practices.

The fact that soap operas never reach a full conclusion has usually been viewed in an entirely negative light. Here are the words of Dennis Porter, who, working from Roland Barthes' theories of narrative structures and ideology, completely condemns soap operas for their failure to resolve all problems:

> Unlike all traditionally end-oriented fiction and drama, soap opera offers process without progression, not a climax and a resolution, but mini-climaxes and provisional denouements that must never be presented in such a way as to eclipse the suspense experienced for associated plot lines. Thus soap opera is the drama of perepetia without anagnorisis. It deals forever in reversals but never portrays the irreversible change which traditionally marks the passage out of ignorance into true knowledge. For actors and audience alike, no action ever stands revealed in the terrible light of its consequences.[44]

These are strange words indeed, coming from one who purports to be analyzing the ideology of narrative form. They are a perfect illustration of how a high art bias, an eagerness to demonstrate the worthlessness of "low" art, can lead us to make claims for high art which we would ordinarily be wary of professing. Terms like "progression," "climax," "resolution," "irreversible change," "true knowledge," and "consequences" are certainly tied to an ideology; they are "linked to classical metaphysics," as Barthes observes. "[The] hermeneutic narrative in which truth predicates an incomplete subject, based on expectation and desire for its imminent closure, is . . . linked to the kerygmatic civilization of meaning and truth, appeal and fulfillment."[45] To criticize classical narrative because, for example, it is based on a suspect notion of progress and then criticize soap opera because it *isn't* will never get us anywhere—certainly not "out of ignorance into true knowledge." A different approach is needed.

Luce Irigaray, describing woman's "rediscovery" of herself, writes, "It is a sort of universe in expansion for which no limits could be fixed and which, for all that, would not be incoherence."[46] The similarities between this description and soap opera as a form are striking. They suggest the possibility that soap operas may not be an entirely negative influence on the viewer; they may also have the force of a *negation*, a negation of the typical (and masculine) modes of pleasure in our society. This challenge, is, moreover, very like the one being mounted in current literary and film theory. Theorists have recently been pointing out the pleasures of the kind of text which breaks the illusion of unity and totality provided the reader or spectator by the "classic text." Hence the emphasis since the structuralists has been on "decentering the subject." But, as we have seen, women are, in their lives, their work, and in certain forms of their pleasure, already decentered—"off center." As Mark Poster remarks in his *Critical Theory of the Family*, "the feeling of being the center of creation is typical of the ego-structure of the bourgeois male."[47] This fact seems to me to be of crucial importance to anyone interested in formulating a feminist aesthetic. Indeed, I would like to argue that soap operas are not altogether at odds with an already developing, though still embryonic, feminist aesthetics.

"Deep in the very nature of soaps is the implied promise that they will last forever."[48] This being the case, a great deal of interest necessarily becomes focused upon those events which retard or impede the flow of the narrative. If, on the one hand, these constant interruptions provide consolation for the housewife's sense of missed opportunities, by illustrating for her the enormous difficulty of getting from desire to fulfillment, on the other hand, the notion of what Porter contemptuously calls "process without progression" is one endorsed by many innovative women artists. In praising Nathalie Sarraute, for example, Mary Ellmann observes that she is not

> interested in the explicit speed of which the novel is capable, only in the nuances which must tend to delay it. In her own discussions of the novel, Nathalie Sarraute is entirely anti-progressive. In criticizing ordinary dialogue, she dislikes its haste: there not being "time" for the person to consider a remark's ramifications, his having to speak and to listen frugally, his having to rush ahead toward his object—which is of course "to order his own conduct."[49]

Soap opera is similarly antiprogressive.[50] Just as Sarraute's work is opposed to the traditional novel form, soap opera is opposed to the classic (male) film narrative, which, with maximum action and minimum, always pertinent dialogue, speeds its way to the restoration of order.

In soap operas, the important thing is that there always be time for a person to consider a remark's ramifications, time for people to speak and to listen lavishly. Actions and climaxes are only of secondary importance. This may seem wilfully to misrepresent soap operas. Certainly they appear to contain a ludicrous number of climaxes and actions: people are always getting blackmailed, having major operations, dying, conducting extra-marital affairs which inevitably result in pregnancy, being kidnapped, going mad, and losing their memories. But just as in real life (one constantly hears it said) it takes a wedding or a funeral to reunite scattered families, so soap opera catastrophes provide convenient occasions for people to come together, confront one another, and explore intense emotions. One advantage of placing people in hospitals, for example, is that because they are immobilized they are forced to take the time to talk to others and listen to what others have to say to them. And friends and family members, imprisoned in waiting rooms (in some ways an apt metaphor for women's homes), can discuss their feelings about the latest tragedy, and, from there, since the waiting often seems interminable, go on to analyze the predicaments of their mutual friends, as well as the state of their own relationships. Thus, in direct contrast to the typical male narrative film, in which the climax functions to resolve difficulties, the "mini-climaxes" of soap opera function to introduce difficulties and to complicate rather than simplify the characters' lives.

Furthermore, as with much women's narrative (such as the fiction of Ivy Compton-Burnett, who strongly influenced Sarraute), dialogue in soap operas is an enormously tricky business. Again, I must take issue with Porter, who says, "Language here is of a kind that takes itself for granted and assumes it is always possible to mean no more and no less than what one intends."[51] More accurately, in soap operas the gap between what is intended and what is actually spoken is often very wide. Secrets better left buried may be blurted out in moments of intensity, or they are withheld just when a character most desires to tell all. This is very different from nighttime television programs and classic Hollywood films with their particularly naive belief in the beneficence of communication. The full revelation of a secret on these shows usually begins or proclaims the restoration of order. Marcus Welby can then get his patient to agree to treatment; Perry Mason can exonerate the innocent and punish the guilty. The necessity of confession, the means through which, according to Michel Foucault, we gladly submit to power, is wholeheartedly endorsed.[52] In soap operas, on the other hand, the effects of confession are often ambiguous, providing relief for some of the characters and dreadful complications for others. (Here too we can see how soap opera melodrama diverges from traditional melodrama, which Peter Brooks, following Eric Bentley, has defined by its impulse to excess, to the overcoming of inhibition and repression: "The genre's very existence is bound to [the] possibility, and necessity, of saying everything.")[53] Moreover, it is remarkable how seldom in soap operas a character can talk another into changing his/her ways. Ordinarily, it takes a major disaster to bring about self-awareness—whereas all Marcus Welby has to do is give his stop-feeling-sorry-for-yourself speech and the character undergoes a drastic personality change. Perhaps more than men, women in our society are aware of the pleasures of language—though less sanguine about its potential use as an instrument of power.

Not only do soap operas suggest an alternate kind of narrative pleasure experienced by women, but they also tell us a great deal about what Johnston calls women's "collective fantasies." To the dismay of many feminist critics, the most powerful fantasy embodied in soap operas appears to be the fantasy of a fully self-sufficient family. Carol Lopate complains:

> Daytime television . . . promises that the family can be everything, if only one is willing to stay inside it. For the woman confined to her house, daytime television fills out the empty spaces of the long day when she is home alone, channels her fantasies toward love and family dramas, and promises her that the life she is in can fulfill her needs. But it does not call to her attention her aloneness and isolation, and it does not suggest to her that it is precisely in her solitude that she has a possibility for gaining a self.[54]

This statement merits close consideration. It implies that the family in soap operas is a mirror-image of the viewer's own family. But for most viewers, this is definitely not the case. What the spectator is looking at and perhaps longing for, is a kind of *extended* family, the direct opposite of her own isolated nuclear family. Most soap operas follow the lives of several generations of a large family, all living in the same town and all intimately involved in one another's lives. The fantasy here is truly a "collective fantasy"—a fantasy of community, but put in terms with which the viewer can be comfortable. Lopate is wrong, I believe, to end her peroration with a call for feminine solitude. For too long women have had too much solitude and, quite rightly, they resent it. In her thought-provoking essay on the family, Barbara Easton points out that since the family is for many women their only support, those women who are abandoned to solitude by feminists eager to undermine this support are apt to turn to the right. People like Anita Bryant and Marabel Morgan, says Easton, "feed on fears of social isolation that have a basis in reality."[55] So do soap operas.

For it is important to recognize that soap opera allays *real* anxieties, satisfies *real* needs and desires, even while it may distort them. The fantasy of community is not only a real desire (as opposed to the "false" ones mass culture is always accused of trumping up), it is a salutary one. As feminists, we have a responsibility to devise ways of meeting these needs that are more creative, honest, and interesting than the ones mass culture has supplied. Otherwise, the search for tomorrow threatens to go on, endlessly.

Afterword

Criticism of mass art can often be a tedious affair. Periodically, a champion of high culture will deplore at great length the decline of taste and sensibility on the part of the reading or viewing public. At least since the publication of Q. D. Leavis's *Fiction and the Reading Public* in 1932 many "high-art" critics have assumed that mass art dulls the mind and renders its consumers unfit to appreciate the beauties of great works. Contrary to what one might expect, Marxist-oriented critics have not taken an entirely different tack. To be sure, they tend to complain of mass art's imposition of "false consciousness" upon the masses, rather than decrying its tendency to debase taste. However, both groups have usually found it necessary when studying mass art to oppose it to high art, thereby demonstrating the political and/or aesthetic superiority of the latter.

Recent continental theory places us in an excellent position to reevaluate the ideas of both Leavis and her followers, and those of the Frankfurt School. Although contemporary theorists have not always drawn out the full implications of their work for the study of mass culture, much of their writing actually contains forceful challenges to commonplace assumptions about the nature of high art and mass art. The Althusserian Pierre Macherey, for example, repudiates the search for structural unity, for "concealed order," in the work of art, arguing instead that

> the order which [the work of art] professes is merely an imagined order, projected on to disorder, the fictive resolution of ideological conflicts, a resolution so precarious that it is obvious in the very letter of the text where incoherence and incompleteness burst forth. It is no longer a question of defects but of indispensable in-

> formers. . . . The work derives its form from this in-
> completeness which enables us to identify the active
> presence of a conflict at its borders. In the defect of the
> work is articulated a new truth.

Macherey's reasoning, taken to its logical conclusion, leads to an extreme position. For when defects are accorded such privileged status, the work of mass art, defective by any traditional aesthetic standard, assumes a kind of superiority to the work of high art. Nevertheless, the new emphasis provides the political critic with what Macherey calls "the revealing form of a knowledge" about the mass cultural text and its consumers.[1]

In this book, for example, I have repeatedly shown the precariousness of the resolutions which are nevertheless so crucial to Harlequin Romances and Gothic novels. In both texts, the transformation of brutal (or, indeed, murderous) men into tender lovers, the insistent denial of the reality of male hostility towards women, point to ideological conflicts so profound that readers must constantly return to the same text (to texts which are virtually the same) in order to be reconvinced. In the chapter on soap operas we saw what amounts to a literal application of Macherey's thesis that "the work derives its form from . . . incompleteness," for in soap operas no attempt is made to project, once and for all, an imagined order on to disorder. The disorder of the form conveys a structure of feeling appropriate to the experience of the woman in the home whose activities and concerns are dispersed and lacking a center. But precisely because of its decentered nature this most discredited genre can be aligned with advanced feminist aesthetics and advanced critical theory as a whole.

Throughout the book I have tended to regard "defects" (that is, what a realist aesthetic would judge to be defects) as "indispensable informers" which reveal the contradictions in women's lives under patriarchy. Textual absences, or the incompleteness of which Macherey speaks, have frequently pointed to the active presence of conflicts at the borders of the works. For instance, some critics have castigated Harlequin Romances for portraying heroines as unbelievably naive, passive, and confused, thus denying the strength and intelligence possessed by many women in real life. However, we saw in this "defect" evidence of various painful psychological dilemmas: e.g., women are supposed to be unconscious of themselves if they are not to incur the charge of narcissism, and yet they are continually forced to look at themselves being looked at. In Gothics, the absence of the mother and the displacement of this figure by various surrogates spoke of the difficulty women experience in coping with their ambivalence towards the first important person in their lives. And in soap operas what concerned us was not the way the television family "mirrored" the modern nuclear family, but the way it necessarily deviated from the norm in order to appear fulfilling. The isolation, solitude, and drudgery of the housewife's world are denied in the creation of a very different world: "Another World."

The idea of contradiction has been crucial to this study—has, in fact, been an informing principle. The concept helps us to understand how certain critics can insist, with some plausibility, on the purely escapist nature of mass art, while others persuasively argue the opposing view that mass art legitimates the status quo. Both sides are partly right; where they err is in regarding the phenomenon as a simple one. Rather than endorsing either of these views, each of my analyses has been predicated on the assumption that mass art not only contains contradictions, it also *functions* in a highly contradictory manner: while appearing to be merely escapist, such art simultaneously challenges and reaffirms traditional values, behavior, and attitudes.

As Richard Dyer points out in his excellent article, "Entertainment and Utopia," mass art appears to be escapist because it "offers the image of 'something better' to escape into, or something we want deeply that our day-to-day lives don't provide."[2] This is the utopian function of entertainment. Dyer lists several aspects of the utopian sensibility most commonly found in mass culture: energy, abundance, intensity, transparency, and community. These terms have obvious relevance to popular narratives for women. The wish for "transparency"—for open, honest, direct, and unambivalent relationship—is perhaps the most urgently expressed desire in all the texts under consideration. I have placed great emphasis throughout this study on the "enigmas" which stimulate questions about people's motives, thoughts, and intentions. I related this emphasis to the dependency of women on men and to the situation of the housewife who must continually be attuned to the moods of her family. Of the other aspects of the utopian sensibility enumerated by Dyer, the wish for community is most strongly evoked by soap operas. I would add to his list the desire for "transcendence" (self-forgetfulness), which is a major current in Harlequin Romances, and the desire for female autonomy, a constant preoccupation of Gothic novels.

However, the utopia envisioned by mass culture is by no means a complete one. As Dyer points out, "the ideals of entertainment imply wants that capitalism itself [and, we might add, patriarchy itself] promises to meet."[3] Therefore, only certain aspirations are admitted by mass art to be valid, while others are ignored or even ridiculed. For example, in Harlequin Romances, the need of women to find meaning and pleasure in activities which are not wholly male-centered such as work or artistic creation is generally scoffed at. Soap operas also undercut, though in subtler fashion, the idea that a woman might obtain satisfaction from these activities. A soap-opera woman might very well be engaged in important work like law or medicine, but even on the job she is likely to be obsessed with her love-life or perhaps actually carrying on her love-life, simultaneously weeping over and operating on the weak heart of her intended. Thus, while popular feminine texts provide outlets for women's dissatisfaction with male-female relationships, they never question the primacy of these relationships. Nor do they overtly question the myth of male superiority or the institutions of marriage and the family. Indeed, patriarchal myths and institutions are, on the manifest level, whole-heartedly embraced, although the anxieties and tensions they give rise to may be said to provoke the need for the texts in the first place.

It is useless to deplore the texts for their omissions, distortions, and conservative affirmations. It is crucial to understand them: to let their very omissions and distortions speak, informing us of the contradictions they are meant to conceal and, equally importantly, of the fears that lie behind them. For the texts often do speak profoundly to us, even those of us who like to think we have shed our "false consciousness" and are actively engaged in challenging patriarchal authority. We cannot rest content with theories which would attribute the texts' popularity to the successful conspiracy of a group of patriarchal capitalists plotting to keep women so happy at home that they remain unwilling to make demands which would greatly restructure the workplace and the family. Such changes are frightening to *most* of us, for they involve an entire reorganization not just of our social lives, but of our psychic lives as well. Given the radical nature of the feminist task, it is no wonder that college students occasionally cut their women's studies classes to find out what is going on in their favorite soap opera. When this happens, it is time for us to stop merely opposing soap operas and to start incorporating them, and other mass-produced feminine fantasies, into our study of women.

Notes

CHAPTER I

1. Virginia Woolf, *A Room of One's Own*, p. 77.
2. Joanna Russ, "What Can A Heroine Do? Or Why Women Can't Write."
3. Roland Barthes, *Roland Barthes*, p. 121. Film theory, in particular, seems to have taken this idea most seriously. See, for example, Janet Bergstrom, "Alternation, Segmentation, Hypnosis: Interview with Raymond Bellour," p. 93.
4. Kenneth Burke, *Language as Symbolic Action*, pp. 352–53.
5. Raymond Williams, *Television*, p. 61.
6. The author of *The Example; or the History of Lucy Cleveland*, quoted in J.M.S. Tompkins, *The Popular Novel in England 1770–1800*, p. 117.
7. George Eliot, "Silly Novels By Lady Novelists."
8. For an example of an article expressing extreme hostility, see Ann Douglas, "Soft-porn Culture." Germaine Greer's chapter on "Romance" in *The Female Eunuch*, pp. 167–85, is a good example of the flippant approach. Most of the many newspaper articles describing women's popular literature are also written in this vein.
9. Ann Douglas, *The Feminization of American Culture*, pp. 2–3.
10. Nina Baym, *Women's Fiction*, p. 29.
11. Herbert Ross Brown, *The Sentimental Novel in America 1789–1860*, p. 289.
12. Eliza Vicery, *Emily Hamilton*, quoted in Brown, p. 38.
13. Tompkins, *The Popular Novel in England*, p. 148.
14. Russ, "What Can a Heroine Do?" p. 7.
15. Quoted in Brown, p. 49.
16. Hannah Webster Foster, *The Coquette* (1797) (New York: Columbia Univ. Press, 1939), p. 41.

17. Tompkins, p. 149.

18. Susanna Rowson, *The Fille de Chambre*, quoted in Brown, p. 48.

19. James Hart, *The Popular Book*, p. 64.

20. Elaine Showalter, *A Literature of Their Own*, p. 160.

21. Brown, p. 282.

22. Hart, p. 106.

23. Helen Waite Papashvily, *All the Happy Endings*, p. xvii.

24. Baym, p. 27.

25. Papashvily, p. 171.

26. Elaine Showalter, "Review Essay: Literary Criticism," p. 435.

27. The term "colonized leisure" is Stanley Aronowitz's. See his *False Promises*, pp. 51–133.

28. The phrase is Hans Magnus Enzensberger's. See *The Consciousness Industry*.

29. Max Horkheimer and Theodor W. Adorno, *Dialectic of Enlightenment*, p. 135.

30. An interesting Marxist critique of the Frankfurt School's position is also advanced by Lillian S. Robinson in her chapter "Criticism: Who Needs It?" in *Sex, Class and Culture*, pp. 69–94.

31. For a full explication of the term "standardization" as it was used by the Frankfurt School, see Theodor W. Adorno, "On Popular Music."

32. Fredric Jameson, "Reification and Utopia in Mass Culture," p. 136.

33. Hans Robert Jauss, "Levels of Identification of Hero and Audience," p. 286.

34. Jameson, p. 141.

35. Jameson, p. 146.

36. The phrase is Stuart Ewen's. See his *Captains of Consciousness*.

37. Leo Spitzer, "American Advertising Explained as Popular Art," in his *Essays on English and American Literature*, p. 263.

38. Louis Althusser, "Ideology and Ideological State Apparatuses," in his *Lenin and Philosophy and Other Essays*, pp. 127–86.

39. Helene Deutsche, *The Psychology of Women*, Vol. II, pp. 105, 245.

40. Douglas, "Soft-porn Culture," p. 28.

41. Herbert Marcuse, *Eros and Civilization*, pp. 127–43.

42. See Enzensberger, p. 110.

43. Herbert Marcuse, *Counterrevolution and Revolt*, p. 92.

44. Jameson, p. 144.

45. Juliet Mitchell's is probably the most extended discussion of Freud's revelance to feminism. See her *Psychoanalysis and Feminism*.

46. Sigmund Freud, "The 'Uncanny.'"

47. See "The Dissolution of the Oedipus Complex."

48. Quoted in Brown, p. 25.

49. Josef Breuer and Sigmund Freud, *Studies on Hysteria*, p. 41.

50. Breuer, p. 46.

51. Carolyn Heilbrun, "Hers," p. C2.

CHAPTER II

1. My information about the Harlequin company comes from two articles: one by Michael Posner, "Harlequin Novels into Motion Pictures," *Macleans*, 20 February 1978, pp. 72–76; the other by Phyllis Berman, "They Call Us Illegitimate," *Forbes*, 6 March 1978, pp. 37–38.

2. No doubt the number of women who actually read Harlequins is greater than these statistics reflect. Many women probably pass on their copies to friends. And enormous quantities of paperback romances are often found in used bookstores.

3. Berman, "They Call Us Illegitimate," p. 38.

4. Russell B. Nye, *The Unembarrassed Muse*, p. 55.

5. *The Writer's 1978 Yearbook*, p. 103.

6. For a more detailed description of the formula, see Kathryn Weibel, *Mirror Mirror*, pp. 32–38.

7. For a detailed, though often frivolous discussion of *Pamela's* influence on popular romantic novels see Robert Palfrey Utter and Gwendolyn Bridges Needham, *Pamela's Daughters*.

8. John Berger, *Ways of Seeing*, p. 46.

9. Germaine Greer, *The Female Eunuch*, p. 176.

10. Susan Brownmiller, *Against Our Will*, p. 360.

11. Greer, p. 178. Ann Barr Snitow also rejects the "reflection theory" of female fantasies in her valuable article, "Mass-Market Romance: Pornography for Women is Different."

12. Clara M. Thompson, *On Women*, p. 133.

13. The term "enigma" is Roland Barthes's. His *S/Z* has

greatly influenced my thinking about the way the romantic narrative purveys its ideological message.

14. Margaret Pargeter, *Hold Me Captive* (Toronto: Harlequin, 1976), p. 35; hereafter cited as *Captive*. Other Harlequin Romances directly referred to in the text are: Helen Bianchin, *Bewildered Haven* (Toronto: Harlequin, 1976) (*Haven*); Katrina Britt, *If Today Be Sweet* (Toronto: Harlequin, 1976) (*Today*); Sheila Douglas, *Sherringdon Hall* (Toronto: Harlequin, 1976) (*Sherringdon*); Elizabeth Hunter, *The Bride Price* (Toronto: Harlequin, 1974) (*Bride*); Pamela Kent, *Enemy Lover* (Toronto: Harlequin, 1964; rpt. 1976) (*Enemy*); Rebecca Stratton, *Chateau D'Armor* (Toronto: Harlequin, 1976) (*Chateau*); Margaret Way, *A Lesson in Loving* (Toronto: Harlequin, 1976) (*Lesson*); Sophie Weston, *Goblin Court* (Toronto: Harlequin, 1976) (*Goblin*).

15. Terry Carr, ex-editor of Ace Books, quoted in Joanna Russ, "Somebody is Trying to Kill Me and I Think It's My Husband: The Modern Gothic," p. 667.

16. Russ, "Somebody is Trying to Kill Me," p. 669.

17. Roland Barthes has noted the same yoking of contraries in descriptions of fashion ("*douces et fières, strictes et tendres,*" etc.). He argues that "these psychological paradoxes testify to a dream of totality according to which the human being can be everything at once and won't have to choose." See *Système de la Mode*, pp. 257–58.

18. Wolfgang Iser, *The Implied Reader*, p. 282.

19. See, for instance, John G. Cawelti, *The Six-Gun Mystique*, p. 21.

20. Brownmiller, p. 424.

21. Roland Barthes, *Mythologies*, p. 150.

22. Barthes, *Mythologies*, p. 42.

23. Samuel Richardson, *Pamela* (Boston: Houghton Mifflin, 1971), p. 214.

24. Karen Horney, *Feminine Psychology*, p. 108.

25. *Pamela*, p. 152.

26. Charlotte Brontë, *Jane Eyre* (New York: Dell, 1961), pp. 309–10.

27. For a more detailed discussion of Brontë's attempt to subvert feminine fantasy see Helene Moglen, *Charlotte Brontë: The Self Conceived*, pp. 105–45.

28. For example, Richard Chase, 'The Brontës: A Centennial Observance."

29. Karl Marx, *Early Writings*, p. 43.

30. Helene Deutsch, *The Psychology of Women*, Vol. I, p. 255.

31. Ian Watt, *The Rise of the Novel*, p. 168.

32. Jane Austen, *Pride and Prejudice* (New York: Perennial Classics, 1965), p. 312.

33. *Pride and Prejudice*, p. 204.

34. Ellen Moers, *Literary Women*, p. 70.

35. Of course, Austen's novel is rich and complex, and I am not suggesting it can be reduced to the elements I have chosen to isolate here. Nevertheless, it is important to point out the ways Austen contributed to the development of the popular romantic formula. Many critics have observed that *Pride and Prejudice* makes use of older conventions (particularly in the seduction of Lydia by Wickham and in the portrayal of Darcy). But no one has considered that Austen may have inaugurated new conventions at the same time that she borrowed from older ones. For illuminating discussions of fictional conventions in *Pride and Prejudice*, see Mary Lascelles, *Jane Austen and Her Art*, esp. pp. 73–75; Marvin Mudrick, *Jane Austen: Irony as Defense and Discovery*, esp. pp. 110–26; and Henrietta Ten Harmsel, *Jane Austen: A Study in Fictional Conventions*, pp. 61–93.

36. *Pamela*, p. 177.

37. Berger, p. 47.

38. Doris Lessing, *Martha Quest* (London: Michael Joseph, 1952), pp. 286–87.

39. *Pamela*, p. 42.

40. Roland Barthes, "An Introduction to the Structural Analysis of Narrative," p. 262.

41. Jonathan Culler, *Structuralist Poetics*, p. 199.

42. Berger, p. 47.

43. Cawelti, p. 11.

44. Howard M. Wolowitz, "Hysterical Character and Feminine Identity," p. 313.

45. Wolowitz, p. 311.

46. Wolowitz, p. 313.

CHAPTER III

1. Quoted in Russ, "Somebody is Trying to Kill Me," p. 667.

2. Weibel, p. 38.

3. Rona Randall, *Dragonmede* (New York: Ballantine,

1974), p. 187. Other Gothic novels directly referred to in the text are: Dorothy Eden, *An Afternoon Walk* (New York: Coward, Mc-Cann & Geoghegan, 1971), hereafter cited as *Afternoon*; Katherine Wigmore Eyre, *Monk's Court* (New York: Appleton-Century, 1966); Victoria Holt, *The King of the Castle* (New York: Fawcett Crest, 1967) (*King*); Victoria Holt, *Menfreya in the Morning* (New York: Fawcett Crest, 1966) (*Menfreya*); Susan Howatch, *The Dark Shore* (New York: Stein and Day, 1965) (*Shore*); Anne Maybury, *Someone Waiting* (New York: Ace, 1961) (*Waiting*); Barbara Michaels, *Ammie, Come Home* (New York: Fawcett Crest, 1968) (*Ammie*); Paula Minton, *Orphan of the Shadows* (New York: Prestige, 1965); Margaret Ritter, *The Lady in the Tower* (New York: Avon, 1972) (*Lady*); Mary Stewart, *Nine Coaches Waiting* (New York: Fawcett Crest, 1958); Phyliss A. Whitney, *Spindrift* (New York: Fawcett Crest, 1976).

4. Quoted in Russ, "Sombody is Trying to Kill Me," p. 667.

5. Russ, "Sombody is Trying to Kill Me," p. 681.

6. Norman A. Cameron, "Paranoid Conditions and Paranoia," p. 682.

7. Alexandra Symonds, "Phobias after Marriage: Women's Declaration of Dependence," p. 290. And David A. Freedman, "On Women Who Hate Their Husbands," pp. 235–37.

8. Cameron, "Paranoid Conditions," p. 682.

9. Sigmund Freud, "Psychoanalytical Notes Upon an Autobiographical Account of a Case of Paranoia."

10. Norman A. Cameron, *The Psychology of Behavior Disorders: A Biosocial Interpretation*. See also Cameron's discussion of paranoia in his *Behavior Pathology*, pp. 372–413.

11. Jane Austen, *Northanger Abbey* (New York: Laurel, 1965), pp. 30–31.

12. Ann Radcliffe, *The Mysteries of Udolpho* (London: Oxford Univ. Press, 1970), p. 491.

13. See Devendra P. Varma, *The Gothic Flame*, pp. 105–7 for a list of these complaints from the nineteenth century to the present.

14. D.W. Swanson, P.J. Bohnert, and J.A. Smith, *The Paranoid*, p. 43.

15. In another context, Edith Birkhead makes much the same point: "Radcliffe deliberately excites trembling apprehensions in order that she may show how absurd they are. We are befooled that she may enjoy a quietly malicious triumph. The result is that

we become wary and cautious." *The Tale of Terror*, p. 51.
16. Cameron, "Paranoid Conditions," p. 683.
17. In other words, the cozy, intimate space of the early home which Gaston Bachelard praises throughout *The Poetics of Space* has become for the woman the "hostile space" of which Bachelard refuses to speak, but of which as feminist critics it is impossible for us *not* to speak. See *The Poetics of Space*, p. xxxii.
18. Cameron, "Paranoid Conditions," p. 683.
19. Russ, "Sombody is Trying to Kill Me," p. 681.
20. Cameron, "Paranoid Conditions," p. 683.
21. W.W. Meissner, *The Paranoid Process*, p. 575.
22. This is a point Meissner continually makes throughout his study.
23. Ellen Moers, *Literary Women*, p. 134.
24. Freedman, "On Women Who Hate Their Husbands," p. 228.
25. *The Mysteries of Udolpho*, p. 112.
26. Freedman, p. 228.
27. Moers, p. 135. Peter Brooks discusses how in the eighteenth century the "idea of the holy" underwent a profound change, as the "sacred" became transformed into terror (in Rudolph Otto's terminology, the *Mysterium tremendum* became pure *tremendum*). Brooks applies these insights to Matthew Lewis' *The Monk*. See "Virtue and Terror: *The Monk*." In women's literature filial piety seems to have undergone a similar transformation. Feelings of love and awe towards the father (which one finds, for example, amply expressed in the works of Fanny Burney) degenerated, in Radcliffe's novels, into emotions primarily consisting of fear and dread.
28. Norman N. Holland and Leona F. Sherman touch upon this point in their discussion, "Gothic Possibilities."
29. Patricia Meyer Spacks, *The Female Imagination*, p. 150.
30. Gertrude R. Ticho, "Female Autonomy and Young Adult Women," p. 153.
31. Ticho, p. 149.
32. *The Mysteries of Udolpho*, p. 366.
33. *Jane Eyre*, p. 271.
34. Russ, "Sombody is Trying to Kill Me," p. 684.
35. Nancy Chodorow, *The Reproduction of Mothering*, p. 103. On this point see also Jane Flax, "The Conflict Between Nurturance and Autonomy in Mother–Daughter Relationships and Within Feminism."

36. Chodorow, p. 191.

37. Freud, "The 'Uncanny,'" p. 144.

38. Gilbert and Gubar, p. 86.

39. Louisa May Alcott, "A Whisper in the Dark," in *Plots and Counterplots: More Unknown Thrillers of Louisa May Alcott*, p. 296.

40. "A Whisper in the Dark," p. 297.

41. Analysts have long recognized this fact. Important early contributions to the development of feminine psychology include Helene Deutsch; Jeanne Lampl-de Groot, "The Evolution of the Oedipus Complex in Women"; and Ernest Jones, "The Early Development of Female Sexuality."

42. Chodorow, p. 121.

43. Meissner, p. 767.

44. Swanson, p. 11.

45. Swanson, p. 14.

46. "Overdetermination" is Freud's concept denoting one aspect of the dream work; it refers to the multiple causation of dream images. See *The Interpretation of Dreams*, esp. pp. 181–82. The term has gained widespread currency through Louis Althusser's use of it. See *For Marx*, pp. 89–116; also 252–53. Also see Juliet Mitchell, *Woman's Estate*, p. 101.

47. Russ, "Somebody is Trying to Kill Me," p. 668.

48. Ruth F. Lax notes that mothering is often based on the "unconscious paradigm: 'I shall be to my child the mother I wanted to have, not the mother I had, who created the condition which resulted in my narcissistic wound.'" "Some Aspects of the Interaction between Mother and Impaired Child: Mother's Narcissistic Trauma," p. 343.

49. Symonds, p. 298.

50. Symonds, p. 299.

51. Symonds, p. 301.

52. Symonds, p. 296–97.

53. Symonds, p. 296. As Kenneth F. Artiss and Dexter M. Bullard observe, "paranoid thinking may well be a weapon of the weak." "Paranoid Thinking in Everyday Life," p. 93.

54. Symonds, p. 292.

55. See Sigmund Freud, "The Most Prevalent Form of Degradation in Erotic Life," pp. 173–86.

56. Meissner, pp. 452–53.

57. Freedman, p. 235. André Green speaks to the same prob-

lem: "The compromise in which a basic fantasy of feminine sexuality might be exemplified is that of Hercules spinning at the feet of Omphale. We find here a typically feminine wish to have constantly at her side the man of her desire in a double role—protecting and virile like the father, and at the same time being used as if he were the mother. Man is feminized here, not so much because the woman wants to castrate him but because she wants to be sure of his *loving, maternal, reassuring* and *undangerous* role." See "Aggression, Femininity, Paranoia and Reality," p. 208.

58. Another study by Robert L. Dupont, Jr. and Henry Grunebaum notes the same phenomenon. See "Willing Victims: The Husbands of Paranoid Women."

59. Freedman, p. 234.

60. Jule Nydes, "The Paranoid-Masochistic Character," *Psychoanalytic Review*, p. 217.

61. Freedman, p. 236.

62. H. Guntrip, quoted in Meissner, p. 529.

63. Meissner, p. 544.

64. Mary Wollstonecraft, *Maria, Or the Wrongs of Woman* (New York: W.W. Norton Co., 1975), p. 74.

65. *Maria*, p. 75.

66. *Maria*, p. 49.

CHAPTER IV

1. Anthony Astrachan, quoted in Dan Wakefield, *All Her Children*, p. 149.

2. Weibel, p. 56.

3. Horace Newcomb, *T.V.: The Most Popular Art*, p. 253.

4. Barthes, *S/Z*, p. 76.

5. Frank Kermode, *The Sense of an Ending*, p. 7.

6. Walter Benjamin, "The Storyteller," in his *Illuminations*, p. 101.

7. Benjamin, "The Storyteller," pp. 100–101.

8. Kermode, p. 162.

9. Papashvily, p. 194.

10. Barbara Easton, "Feminism and the Contemporary Family," p. 30.

11. Not only can women count on a never ending story line, they can also, to a great extent, rely upon the fact that their favorite

characters will never desert them. To take a rather extreme example: when, on one soap opera, the writers killed off a popular female character and viewers were unhappy, the actress was brought back to portray the character's twin sister. See Madeleine Edmondson and David Rounds, *From Mary Noble to Mary Hartman: The Complete Soap Opera Book*, p. 208.

12.   Dennis Porter, "Soap Time: Thoughts on a Commodity Art Form," p. 783.

13.   Edmondson and Rounds, *The Complete Soap Opera Book*, pp. 104–110.

14.   Barthes, *S/Z*, p. 135.

15.   John G. Cawelti, *Adventure, Mystery and Romance*, pp. 45–46.

16.   Laura Mulvey, "Visual Pleasure and Narrative Cinema," p. 420.

17.   Mulvey, p. 420.

18.   Mulvey, p. 420.

19.   Edmondson and Rounds, p. 193.

20.   See Paul Mayer, "Creating 'Ryan's Hope.'"

21.   Robert B. Heilman, *Tragedy and Melodrama*, p. 85.

22.   There are still villains on soap operas, but their numbers have declined considerably since radio days—to the point where they are no longer indispensable to the formula. "The Young and the Restless," for example, does without them.

23.   According to Weibel, we quite simply "deplore" the victimizers and totally identify with the victim (p. 62).

24.   "A soap opera without a bitch is a soap opera that doesn't get watched. The more hateful the bitch the better. Erica of 'All My Children' is a classic. If you want to hear some hairy rap, just listen to a bunch of women discussing Erica.

'Girl, that Erica needs her tail whipped.'

'I wish she'd try to steal my man and plant some marijuana in my purse. I'd be mopping up the street with her new hairdo.'" Bebe Moore Campbell, "Hooked on Soaps," p. 103.

25.   Dorothy Dinnerstein, *The Mermaid and The Minotaur*, p. 236.

26.   "The author, Mary Elizabeth Braddon, belonged to that class of writers called by Charles Reade 'obstacles to domestic industry.'" Frank Rahill, *The World of Melodrama*, p. 204.

27.   Elaine Showalter, *A Literature of Their Own*, p. 204.

28.   Mary Ellmann, *Thinking About Women*, p. 181. Molly

Haskell makes a similar point in her discussion of "The Woman's Film," in *From Reverence to Rape*, pp. 172–73.

29. The game, observed by Freud, in which the child plays "disappearance and return" with a wooden reel tied to a string. "What he did was to hold the reel by the string and very skilfully throw it over the edge of his curtained cot, so that it disappeared into it, at the same time uttering his expressive 'O-O-O-O'. [Freud speculates that this represents the German word *'fort'* or *'gone.'*] He then pulled the reel out of the cot again by the string and hailed its reappearance with a joyful 'da' ['there']." According to Freud, "Throwing away the object so that it was 'gone' might satisfy an impulse of the child's, which was suppressed in his actual life, to revenge himself on his mother for going away from him. In that case it would have a defiant meaning: 'All right then, go away! I don't need you. I'm sending you away myself.'" Sigmund Freud, *Beyond the Pleasure Principle*, pp. 10–11.

30. Speaking of the child's *fort-da* game, Freud notes, "At the outset he was in a passive situation—he was overpowered by experience; but by repeating it, unpleasurable though it was, as a game, he took on an *active* part. These efforts might be put down to an instinct for mastery that was acting independently of whether the memory was in itself pleasurable or not." In *Beyond the Pleasure Principle*, p. 10.

31. Jean-Paul Sartre's phrase for the tension surrealism's created object sets up in the spectator is remarkably appropriate here. See *What is Literature?*, p. 133n.

32. Marsha Kinder, "Review of *Scenes from a Marriage*," p. 51.

33. Chodorow, p. 179.

34. Porter, p. 786.

35. Tillie Olsen, *Silences*, pp. 18–19.

36. Williams, p. 95.

37. Benjamin, "On Some Motifs in Baudelaire," in *Illuminations*, p. 176.

38. Benjamin, "What is Epic Theater?" in *Illuminations*, p. 151.

39. See Sherry B. Ortner's brilliant discussion of women's position in culture, "Is Female to Male as Nature Is to Culture?"

40. Benjamin, "The Work of Art in the Age of Mechanical Reproduction," in *Illuminations*, p. 240.

41. Edmondson and Rounds, pp. 46–47.

42. Benjamin, "The Work of Art," pp. 239–40.

43. Claire Johnston, "Women's Cinema as Counter-Cinema," p. 217.

44. Porter, pp. 783–84.

45. Barthes, *S/Z*, p. 45.

46. Luce Irigaray, "Ce sexe qui n'en est pas un," p. 104.

47. Mark Poster, *Critical Theory of the Family*, p. 9.

48. Edmondson and Rounds, p. 112.

49. Ellmann, pp. 222–23.

50. As David Grimsted points out, melodrama may always have been deeply antiprogressive, in spite of its apparent hopefulness and thrust toward a happy ending. First, the "centrality of the villain in these plays, even though he was always eventually defeated, suggested a world where the evil and terror of which he was an incarnation were constant threats." And second, in classic melodrama (as in soap operas), virtue is always allied with the past—with fathers, mothers, rural life styles, etc., while the present is conceived of as dangerous, confusing and perhaps even "degenerate." See *Melodrama Unveiled*, pp. 223–24.

51. Porter, p. 788.

52. Michel Foucault, *The History of Sexuality*, esp. pp. 57–73. In this connection, it is interesting to recall how in many detective stories, T.V. shows, and films, the detective must overcome the reluctance of an *innocent* party to yield some bit of information necessary to the solution of the crime. For an interesting discussion of Dragnet's Joe Friday as the Great Listener, see Reuel Denney, *The Astonished Muse*, pp. 82–92.

53. Peter Brooks, *The Melodramatic Imagination*, p. 42. Or, as Eric Bentley puts it, "melodrama is not so much the exaggerated as the uninhibited." See *The Life of the Drama*, p. 206.

54. Carol Lopate, "Daytime Television: You'll Never Want to Leave Home," p. 51.

55. Easton, p. 34.

Afterword

1. Pierre Macherey, *A Theory of Literary Production*, pp. 155–56.

2. Richard Dyer, "Entertainment and Utopia," p. 177.

3. Dyer, pp. 184–85.

Bibliography

Adorno, Theodor W. (with the assistance of George Simpson). "On Popular Music." *Studies in Philosophy and Social Science* 9, no. 1 (1941), pp. 17–48.

Althusser, Louis. *For Marx*. Translated by Ben Brewster. New York: Vintage Books, 1970.

———. *Lenin and Philosophy and Other Essays*. New York: Monthly Review Press, 1971.

Arnheim, Rudolph. "The World of the Daytime Serial." In *Radio Research*. Edited by Paul F. Lazarsfeld and Frank N. Stanton. New York: Essential Books, 1942–43.

Aronowitz, Stanley. *False Promises: The Shaping of American Working Class Consciousness*. New York: McGraw-Hill, 1964.

Artiss, Kenneth and Bullard, Dexter M. "Paranoid Thinking in Everyday Life." *Archives of General Psychiatry* 14 (1966): 89–93.

Bachelard, Gaston. *The Poetics of Space*. Translated by Maria Jolas. Boston: Beacon Press, 1969.

Barthes, Roland. "An Introduction to the Structural Analysis of Narrative." Translated by Lionel Duisit. *New Literary History* 6 (1975): 236–72.

———. *Mythologies*. Translated by Annette Lavers. New York: Hill and Wang, 1972.

———. *The Pleasure of the Text*. Translated by Richard Miller. New York: Hill and Wang, 1975.

———. *Roland Barthes*. Translated by Richard Howard. New York: Hill and Wang, 1977.

———. *S/Z*. Translated by Richard Miller. New York: Hill and Wang, 1974.

———. *Système de la Mode*. Paris: Éditions Du Seuil, 1967.

Baym, Nina. *Women's Fiction: A Guide to Novels by and about Women in America, 1820–1870*. Ithaca, N.Y.: Cornell University Press, 1978.

Ben-Horin, Daniel. "Television Without Tears: An Outline of a Socialist Approach to Popular Television." *Socialist Review* 35 (1977): 7–35.

Benjamin, Walter. *Illuminations.* Translated by Harry Zohn. Edited by Hannah Arendt. New York: Schocken Books, 1969.

———. *Understanding Brecht.* Translated by Anna Bostock. London: New Left Books, 1973.

Bentley, Eric. *The Life of the Drama.* New York: Atheneum, 1974.

Berger, John. *Ways of Seeing.* New York: The Viking Press, 1973.

Bergstrom, Janet. "Alternation, Segmentation, Hypnosis: Interview with Raymond Bellour." *Camera Obscura* 3/4, pp. 71–103.

Birkhead, Edith. *The Tale of Terror: A Study of Gothic Romance.* New York: Russell & Russell, 1921.

Boorstin, Daniel J. *The Image: A Guide to Pseudo-events in America.* New York: Atheneum, 1971.

Booth, Wayne C. *The Rhetoric of Fiction.* Chicago: University of Chicago Press, 1961.

Breuer, Josef and Freud, Sigmund. *Studies on Hysteria.* In *The Standard Edition of the Complete Psychological Works of Sigmund Freud.* Translated by James Strachey. 24 vols. Vol. 2. London: The Hogarth Press, 1953–74.

Brooks, Peter. *The Melodramatic Imagination: Balzac, Henry James, Melodrama, and the Mode of Excess.* New Haven: Yale University Press, 1976.

———. "Virtue and Terror: *The Monk*." *ELH* 40 (1973): 249–63.

Brown, Herbert Ross. *The Sentimental Novel in America, 1789–1860.* Durham, N.C.: Duke University Press, 1940.

Brownmiller, Susan. *Against Our Will: Men, Women and Rape.* New York: Bantam Books, 1976.

Burke, Kenneth. *Language as Symbolic Action: Essays on Life, Literature, and Method.* Berkeley: University of California Press, 1973.

Cameron, Norman A. "Paranoid Conditions and Paranoia." In *American Handbook of Psychiatry.* 2nd ed. Edited by Silvano Arieti. New York: Basic Books, 1974.

———. *The Psychology of Behavior Disorders: A Biosocial Interpretation.* Boston: Houghton Mifflin, 1947.

———. *Behavior Pathology.* Boston: Houghton Mifflin, 1951.

Campbell, Bebe Moore. "Hooked on Soaps." *Essence,* November 1978, pp. 100–103.

Cawelti, John G. *Adventure, Mystery, and Romance.* Chicago: University of Chicago Press, 1976.

———. *The Six-Gun Mystique.* Bowling Green, Ohio: Bowling Green University Popular Press, n.d.

Chase, Richard. "The Brontës: A Centennial Observance." *Kenyon Review* 9 (Autumn 1947): 486–506.

Chodorow, Nancy, *The Reproduction of Mothering: Psychoanalysis and the Sociology of Gender.* Berkeley: University of California Press, 1978.

Culler, Jonathan. *Structuralist Poetics.* London: Routledge & Kegan Paul, 1975.

Deer, Irving and Deer, Harriet, eds. *The Popular Arts: A Critical Reader.* New York: Charles Scribner's Sons, 1967.

Denney, Reuel. *The Astonished Muse.* Chicago: University of Chicago Press, 1957.

Deutsch, Helene. *The Psychology of Women.* 2 vols. New York: Grune & Stratton, 1944–45.

Dinnerstein, Dorothy. *The Mermaid and the Minotaur: Sexual Arrangements and Human Malaise.* New York: Harper & Row, 1976.

Douglas, Ann. *The Feminization of American Culture.* New York: Avon Books, 1978.

———. "Soft-porn Culture." *New Republic,* 30 August 1980, pp. 25–29.

Downing, Mildred. "Heroines of the Daytime Serial." *Journal of Communication* 24 (1974): 130–37.

Dupont, Robert L., Jr. and Grunebaum, Henry. "Willing Victims: The Husbands of Paranoid Women." *American Journal of Psychiatry* 125 (1968): 151–59.

Dyer, Richard. "Entertainment and Utopia." In *Genre: The Musical: A Reader.* Edited by Rick Altman. London: Routledge & Kegan Paul, 1981.

Easton, Barbara. "Feminism and the Contemporary Family." *Socialist Review* 8, no. 3 (1978), pp. 11–36.

Edmondson, Madeleine. "Confessions of a Soap Addict." *Newsweek,* 22 August 1977, p. 3.

——— and Rounds, David. *From Mary Noble to Mary Hartman: The Complete Soap Opera Book.* New York: Stein and Day, 1976.

Eliot, George. "Silly Novels by Lady Novelists." *Westminster Review* 64 (1856): 442–61.

Ellmann, Mary. *Thinking about Women*. New York: Harvest Books, 1968.

Enzensberger, Hans Magnus. *The Consciousness Industry: On Literature, Politics and the Media*. New York: Continuum Books, 1974.

Ewen, Stuart. *Captains of Consciousness: Advertising and the Social Roots of the Consumer Culture*. New York: McGraw-Hill, 1976.

Flax, Jane. "The Conflict Between Nurturance and Autonomy in Mother-Daughter Relationships and Within Feminism." *Feminist Studies* 4 (1978): 171–89.

Foucault, Michel. *The History of Sexuality: Volume I: An Introduction*. Translated by Robert Hurley. New York: Vintage Books, 1980.

Freedman, David A. "On Women Who Hate Their Husbands." In *Psychoanalysis and Female Sexuality*. Edited by Hendrick M. Ruitenbeek. New Haven, Conn.: College & University Press, 1966.

Freud, Sigmund. *Beyond the Pleasure Principle*. Translated by James Strachey. New York: W.W. Norton Co., 1961.

———. "The Dissolution of the Oedipus Complex." In *Standard Edition of the Complete Psychological Works*. Translated by James Strachey. 24 vols. Vol. 19. London: Hogarth Press, 1953–74.

———. "Female Sexuality." In *Standard Edition of the Complete Psychological Works*. Vol. 21.

———. "Femininity." In *Standard Edition of the Complete Psychological Works*. Vol. 22.

———. "Some Psychical Consequences of the Anatomical Distinction Between the Sexes." In *Standard Edition of the Complete Psychological Works*. Vol. 19.

———. *The Interpretation of Dreams*. Translated by James Strachey. New York: Avon Books, 1971.

———. "The Most Prevalent Form of Degradation in Erotic Life." In *On Creativity and the Unconscious: Papers on the Psychology of Art, Literature, Love, Religion*. Edited by Benjamin Nelson. New York: Harper Torchbooks, 1958.

———. "Some Character-Types Met With in Psycho-Analytic Work." In *On Creativity and the Unconscious: Papers on the Psychology of Art, Literature, Love, Religion*.

———. "The 'Uncanny.'" In *On Creativity and the Unconscious:*

Papers on the Psychology of Art, Literature, Love, Religion.
———. "Notes Upon an Autobiographical Account of a Case of Paranoia (*Dementia Paranoides*)." In *Three Case Histories.* Edited by Philip Rieff. New York: Collier Books, 1973.

Gans, Herbert J. *Popular Culture and High Culture: An Analysis and Evaluation of Taste.* New York: Basic Books, 1974.

Gilbert, Sandra M. and Gubar, Susan. *The Madwoman in the Attic: The Woman Writer and the Nineteenth-Century Literary Imagination.* New Haven, Conn.: Yale University Press, 1979.

Green, André. "Aggression, Femininity, Paranoia and Reality." *International Journal of Psycho-Analysis* 53 (1972): 205–11.

Greer, Germaine. *The Female Eunuch.* New York: McGraw-Hill, 1971.

Grimsted, David. *Melodrama Unveiled: American Theater and Culture, 1800–1850.* Chicago: University of Chicago Press, 1968.

Hall, Stuart and Whannel, Paddy. *The Popular Arts.* New York: Pantheon Books, 1965.

Hart, James D. *The Popular Book: A History of America's Literary Taste.* New York: Oxford University Press, 1950.

Haskell, Molly. *From Reverence to Rape: The Treatment of Women in the Movies.* New York: Penguin, 1974.

Heilbrun, Carolyn G. "Hers." *The New York Times,* 26 February 1981, p. C2.

Heilman, Robert B. *Tragedy and Melodrama: Versions of Experience.* Seattle: University of Washington Press, 1968.

Herzog, Herta. "What Do We Really Know about Daytime Serial Listeners?" In *Radio Research.* Edited by Paul F. Lazarsfeld and Frank N. Stanton. New York: Essential Books, 1942–43.

Hoggart, Richard. *The Uses of Literacy.* Fairlawn, N.J.: Essential Books, 1957.

Holland, Norman N. *The Dynamics of Literary Response.* New York: Oxford University Press, 1968.

——— and Sherman, Leona F. "Gothic Possibilities." *New Literary History* 8 (1977): 279–94.

Horkheimer, Max. "Art and Mass Culture." *Studies in Philosophy and Social Science* 9, no. 2 (1941), pp. 290–304.

——— and Adorno, Theodor W. *Dialectic of Enlightenment.* Translated by John Cumming. New York: Continuum Books, 1969.

Horney, Karen. *Feminine Psychology*. New York: W.W. Norton Co., 1973.

Irigaray, Luce. "Ce sexe qui n'en est pas un." In *New French Feminisms*. Edited by Elaine Marks and Isabelle Courtivron. Amherst: University of Massachusetts Press, 1980.

Iser, Wolfgang. *The Implied Reader: Patterns of Communication in Prose Fiction from Bunyan to Beckett*. Baltimore: Johns Hopkins University Press, 1974.

Jacobson, Edith. "The 'Exceptions': An Elaboration of Freud's Character Study." *Psychoanalytic Study of the Child* 14 (1959): 135–54.

Jameson, Fredric. *Marxism and Form: Twentieth Century Dialectical Theories of Literature*. Princeton: Princeton University Press, 1971.

———. "Reification and Utopia in Mass Culture." *Social Text* 1 (1979): 130–48.

Jauss, Hans Robert. "Levels of Identification of Hero and Audience." *New Literary History* 5 (1974): 283–317.

Jay, Martin. *The Dialectical Imagination: A History of the Frankfurt School and the Institute of Social Research, 1923–1950*. Boston: Little, Brown, and Co., 1973.

Johnson R.E., Jr. "The Dialogue of Novelty and Repetition: Structure in 'All My Children.'" *Journal of Popular Culture* 10 (1976): 560–70.

Johnston, Claire. "Women's Cinema as Counter-Cinema." In *Movies and Methods*. Edited by Bill Nichols. Berkeley: University of California Press, 1976.

Jones, Ernest. "The Early Development of Female Sexuality." *International Journal of Psycho-Analysis* 8 (1927): 459–72.

Kaplan, Frank I. "Intimacy and Conformity in American Soap Opera." *Journal of Popular Culture* 9 (1975): 622–25.

Kellner, Douglas. "T.V., Ideology and Emancipatory Popular Culture." *Socialist Review* 45 (1979): 13–53.

Kermode, Frank. *The Sense of an Ending: Studies in the Theory of Fiction*. New York: Oxford University Press, 1967.

Kinder, Marsha. Review of *Scenes from a Marriage*, by Ingmar Bergman. *Film Quarterly* 28, no. 2 (1974–75), pp. 48–53.

LaGuardia, Robert. *The Wonderful World of TV Soap Operas*. New York: Ballantine Books, 1974.

Lampl-de Groot, Jeanne. "The Evolution of the Oedipus Complex in Women." *International Journal of Psycho-Analysis* 9

(1928): 332–45.

Lascelles, Mary. *Jane Austen and Her Art*. London: Oxford University Press, 1939.

Lax, Ruth F. "Some Aspects of the Interaction Between Mother and Impaired Child: Mother's Narcissistic Trauma." *International Journal of Psycho-Analysis* 53 (1972): 339–44.

Lazere, Donald. "Mass Culture, Political Consciousness, and English Studies." *College English* 38 (1977): 751–67.

Leavis, Queenie D. *Fiction and the Reading Public*. London: Chatto & Windus, 1932.

Lefebvre, Henri. *Everyday Life in the Modern World*. Translated by Sacha Rabinovitch. New York: Harper Torchbooks, 1971.

Lesser, Simon O. *Fiction and the Unconscious*. Boston: Beacon Press, 1957.

Lopate, Carol. "Daytime Television: You'll Never Want to Leave Home." *Radical America* 2 (1977): 33–51.

Lowenthal, Leo: *Literature, Popular Culture and Society*. Englewood Cliffs, N.J.: Prentice Hall, 1961.

MacAndrew, Elizabeth and Gorsky, Susan. "Why Do They Faint and Die: The Birth of the Delicate Heroine." *Journal of Popular Culture* 8 (1975): 735–45.

Macdonald, Dwight, *Against the American Grain*. New York: Random House, 1962.

Marcherey, Pierre. *A Theory of Literary Production*. Translated by Geoffrey Wall. London: Routledge & Kegan Paul, 1978.

Marcuse, Herbert. *Eros and Civilization: A Philosophical Inquiry into Freud*. New York: Vintage Books, 1962.

———. *One Dimensional Man: Studies in the Ideology of Advanced Industrial Society*. Boston: Beacon Press, 1964.

———. *Counterrevolution and Revolt*. Boston: Beacon Press, 1972.

Marx, Karl. *Early Writings*. Edited and translated by T.B. Bottomore. New York: McGraw-Hill, 1963.

Mayer, Paul. "Creating 'Ryan's Hope.'" In *T.V. Book*. Edited by Judy Fireman. New York: Workman Publishing Co., 1977.

Meissner, William W. *The Paranoid Process*. New York: Jason Aronson, 1978.

Mendelsohn, Harold. *Mass Entertainment*. New Haven, Conn.: College & University Press, 1966.

Mitchell, Juliet. *Psychoanalysis and Feminism*. New York: Vintage Books, 1975.

133

————. *Woman's Estate.* New York: Vintage Books, 1973.

Moers, Ellen. *Literary Women.* Garden City, N.Y.: Doubleday & Co., 1976.

Moglen, Helene. *Charlotte Brontë: The Self Conceived.* New York: W.W. Norton Co., 1976.

Mudrick, Marvin. *Jane Austen: Irony as Defense and Discovery.* Berkeley: University of California Press, 1968.

Mulvey, Laura. "Visual Pleasure and Narrative Cinema." In *Women and the Cinema.* Edited by Karyn Kay and Gerald Peary. New York: E.P. Dutton, 1977.

Newcomb, Horace, ed. *Television: The Critical View.* New York: Oxford University Press, 1976.

————. *T.V.: The Most Popular Art.* New York: Anchor Books, 1974.

Nydes, Jule. "The Paranoid-Masochistic Character." *Psychoanalytic Review* 50 (1963): 215–51.

Nye, Russell B. *The Unembarassed Muse: The Popular Arts in America.* New York: The Dial Press, 1970.

Olsen, Tillie. *Silences.* New York: Dell Publishing Co., 1979.

Ortega y Gasset. *The Revolt of the Masses.* New York: Mentor Books, 1950.

Ortner, Sherry B. "Is Female to Male as Nature Is to Culture?" In *Woman, Culture and Society.* Edited by Michelle Zimbalist Rosaldo and Louise Lamphere. Stanford, Ca.: Stanford University Press, 1974.

Palter, Ruth. "Radio's Attraction for Housewives." *Hollywood Quarterly* 3 (1948): 248–57.

Papashvily, Helen Waite. *All the Happy Endings, A Study of the Domestic Novel in America, the Women Who Wrote It, the Women Who Read It, in the Nineteenth Century.* New York: Harper & Brothers, 1956.

Porter, Dennis. "Soap Time: Thoughts on a Commodity Art Form." *College English* 38 (1977): 782–88.

Poster, Mark. *Critical Theory of the Family.* New York: Continuum Books, 1978.

Rahill, Frank. *The World of Melodrama.* University Park: Pennsylvania State University Press, 1967.

Real, Michael R. *Mass-Mediated Culture.* Englewood Cliffs, N.J.: Prentice-Hall, 1977.

Rich, Adrienne. "*Jane Eyre*: Temptations of a Motherless Woman." *Ms*, October 1973, pp. 68–72, 98, 106–107.

Robinson, Lillian S. *Sex, Class, and Culture*. Bloomington, Ind.: Indiana University Press, 1978.

Rosenberg, Bernard and White, David Manning, eds. *Mass Culture: The Popular Arts in America*. New York: The Free Press, 1957.

Russ, Joanna. "Somebody Is Trying to Kill Me and I Think It's My Husband: The Modern Gothic." *Journal of Popular Culture* 6 (1973): 666–91.

———. "What Can a Heroine Do? Or Why Women Can't Write." In *Images of Women in Fiction*. Edited by Susan Koppelman Cornillon. Bowling Green, Ohio: Bowling Green University Popular Press, 1972.

Sartre, Jean-Paul. *What Is Literature?* Translated by Bernard Frechtman. New York: Washington Square Press, 1966.

Seldes, Gilbert. *The Seven Lively Arts*. New York: Sagamore Press, 1957.

Showalter, Elaine. "Review Essay: Literary Criticism." *Signs* 1 (1975): 435–60.

———. *A Literature of Their Own*. Princeton: Princeton University Press, 1977.

Snitow, Ann Barr. "Mass Market Romance: Pornography for Women is Different." *Radical History Review* 19 (1979): 141–61.

Spacks, Patricia Meyer. *The Female Imagination*. New York: Alfred A. Knopf, 1975.

Spitzer, Leo. *Essays on English and American Literature*. Princeton: Princeton University Press, 1962.

Swanson, David W.; Bohnert, Philip J.; and Smith, Jackson A. *The Paranoid*. Boston: Little, Brown, and Co., 1970.

Symonds, Alexandra. "Phobias After Marriage: Women's Declaration of Dependence." In *Psychoanalysis and Women*. Edited by Jean Baker Miller. New York: Penguin, 1978.

Ten Harmsell, Henrietta. *Jane Austen: A Study in Fictional Conventions*. The Hague: Mouton, 1964.

Thompson, Clara M. *On Women*. New York: Mentor Books, 1971.

Ticho, Gertrude R. "Female Autonomy and Young Adult Women." In *Female Psychology: Contemporary Analytic Views*. Edited by Harold P. Blum. New York: International Universities Press, 1977.

Tompkins, Joyce M.S. *The Popular Novel in England, 1770–1800*.

Lincoln, Neb.: The University of Nebraska Press, 1961.

Utter, Robert Palfrey and Needham, Gwendolyn Bridges. *Pamela's Daughters*. New York: Macmillan, 1936.

Varma, Devendra P. *The Gothic Flame, Being a History of the GOTHIC NOVEL in England: Its Origins, Efflorescence, Disintegration, and Residuary Influences.* New York: Russell & Russell, 1957.

Wakefield, Dan. *All Her Children.* Garden City, N.Y.: Doubleday & Co., 1976.

Warshow, Robert. *The Immediate Experience: Movies, Comics, Theatre and Other Aspects of Popular Culture.* Garden City, N.Y.: Doubleday & Co., 1962.

Watt, Ian. *The Rise of the Novel: Studies in Defoe, Richardson and Fielding.* Berkeley: University of California Press, 1957.

Weibel, Kathryn. *Mirror Mirror: Images of Women Reflected in Popular Culture.* Garden City, N.Y.: Anchor Books, 1977.

Williams, Raymond. *Culture and Society, 1780–1950.* New York: Columbia University Press, 1958.

———. "Communications as Cultural Science." In *Approaches to Popular Culture.* Edited by C.W.E. Bigsby. Bowling Green, Ohio: Bowling Green University Popular Press, 1976.

———. *Communications.* Rev. ed. New York: Barnes & Noble, 1967.

———. *Television: Technology and Cultural Form.* New York: Schocken Books, 1975.

Wolowitz, Howard M. "Hysterical Character and Feminine Identity." In *Readings on the Psychology of Women.* Edited by Judith M. Bardwick. New York: Harper & Row, 1972.

Woolf, Virginia. *A Room of One's Own.* New York: Harbinger Books, 1957.

Index

137